INSIGHTS ON LIFE

By Russ Ulmer

Insights Publishing

Much of the material in Insights books is by unknown authors, has been contributed by readers and is presented here with the spirit of sharing for strict personal use: with friends, family, or co-workers--to pass it on. Insights Publishing attempts to attribute all credits, where available, to material in this book.

ISBN: 978-0-9793313-0-5

First Printing 2026

Printed in the USA by Insights Publishing

CONTENTS

INTRODUCTION

What is *Insights on Life*? It's a simple collection of quotes, stories, and little anecdotes. Some of them are humorous and some are of a more serious nature. My hope is that they can provide you with enjoyment as well as inspiration. I have been collecting these for years and thought they should be put together in a book. After looking more closely at them I noticed that the common denominator was *life,* or at least some phase of life. So I decided to group them into to the different phases of life that were most appropriate for the selection.

Life - Man has debated the meaning of life for centuries. I'm sorry but this book isn't going to provide you with any earth-shattering answers. However if I had to sum up life with one passage it would be *"Golden Rules for Living*". This is my favorite passage from this chapter and possibly in the entire book. It can provide you with some simple, yet powerful ways of looking at and dealing with life.

Childhood – We all have to start out life as a child and this is probably the most appropriate way to start this book. Children can be the source of many of our joys, and they can also be the source of much of our stress as well. I hope you enjoy this chapter as much as I enjoyed putting it together. I have found some of the entries to be very funny.

Learning – Life is learning and I found this to be the most appropriate chapter to follow childhood. When thinking back on my childhood I inevitably think back on my school days. This chapter includes many little tid bits on teaching and learning that should be enjoyable to those who teach as well as those that have learned.

Fatherhood – For a man there is nothing like that of being a father. Being a father of two children I enjoyed researching and gathering the quotes that I've listed here. I didn't have too much material in this chapter, but I feel that what I do have is very powerful, especially the passage on "*How much do you earn?*" This is one that every father should read.

Motherhood – You can't have a chapter on fatherhood without giving mothers equal time. Just kidding. This chapter was as enjoyable to put together as the chapter on fatherhood. You'll find most of them to be very humorous, however I think you'll enjoy "*Is Heaven in the Yellow Pages.*"

Friends – For most of us spend our lives surrounded by friends. From early childhood, through our school years and on into adulthood, we can't help living our lives without developing relationships with the people around us. Often friendships come and go and sometimes we may have the rare instance of having a close friendship that lasts from early childhood on into our adult years. Friendship is a vital part of our life. We rely on our friends to be our sounding boards and to be there for us in our time of need. Cherish your friends and remember the friendships that you've had.

Love and Happiness – I originally had these divided into two chapters and decided to combine them because of their natural tendency to go hand in hand. If I had to speculate on the meaning of life I would probably sum it up with love and happiness. Love yourself and others and seek happiness for yourself and make others happy.

Work and Success - Some people live their lives based on their desire to be successful. They measure that success in the work that they do. Often it's defined by how much money they earn and by the possessions they obtain. Because of all of this, work is status. Go to a dinner party or to a high school reunion. Count how many times you are asked, "What do you do?" We often compare ourselves with others by the work that we do.

Stress and Change - The one thing that I've learned about life is that change is constant. Life can be stressful, More for some and less for others. We all handle stress and change differently

Spirituality – A book on life would not be complete without something on spirituality for we are all spiritual beings. Spirituality is individual and is as different to each of us as we are with each other. I made it a point to include quotes form two of the most spiritual people of all time, Jesus Christ and Buddha. Although they lived over 5 centuries apart their teachings are very similar.

Growing Older - The one common link in all of us is that we all grow older. Hopefully we will grow wiser at the same time.

Wisdom – I would hope that the one thing we gain as we grow older is wisdom. I have included quotes and insights from Thoreau, Emerson, and Twain. I have also included some wisdom and thoughts that are of a humorous nature.

Most of the selections in this book are from unknown authors. I have researched the material and have not located the original authors for some of the material. If you are the author of any of these selections, please let me know so I can give credit where credit is due.

Enjoy Life!

- 1 -
LIFE

The best things in life are not things.
Unknown

QUOTES ABOUT LIFE

Life is really fun, if we only give it a chance.
Tim Hansel

Don't forget until too late that the business of life is not business but living.
B.C. Forbes

If I had my whole life to live over again, I don't think I'd have the strength.
Flip Wilson

Never lose sight of the fact that just being is fun.
Katherine Hepburn

When the days are too short chances are you are living at your best.
Earl Nightingale

I've developed a new philosophy. I only dread life one day at a time.
Charlie brown (Charles Schultz)

Life is like a box of chocolates.
Forrest Gump

Life is like a ten speed bike. Most of us have gears we never use.
Charles Schultz

Remember, life is not what happens to you but what you make of what happens to you. Everyone dies, but not everyone fully lives. Too many people are having "near-life experiences."
Anonymous

If you're too busy to enjoy life, you're too busy.
Jeff Davidson

Life is a paradise for those who love many things with a passion.
Leo Buscaglia

Nobody gets to live life backward. Look ahead – that's where the future lies.
Ann Landers

We make a living by what we get, but we make a life by what we give.
Winston Churchill

The first step to getting the things you want out of life is this: Decide what you want.
Ben Stein

Life is too important to take seriously.
Corky Siegel

It's not true that life is one damn thing after another; it is one damn thing over and over.
Edna St. Vincent Millay

Life is pleasant. Death is peaceful. It's the transition that's troublesome.
Isaac Asimov

Life is a long lesson in humility.
James M. Barrie

Life is what happens to you while you're busy making other plans.
John Lennon

Life is just a bowl of pits.
Rodney Dangerfield

Life is just a mirror, and what you see out there, you must first see inside of you.
Wally 'Famous' Amos

CULTIVATE YOUR GRATITUDE
FROM A to Z
By RUSS ULMER

Pay **A**ttention
Have **B**alance in your life
Have **C**ompassion for others
Open your eyes to **D**iscovery
You get what you **E**xpect
Family is important
Gratitude is an attitude
Happiness is inside you
Don't lose your **I**magination
Celebrate the **J**oy of others
Keep it positive
Love yourself
Money is not wealth
Nobody's perfect
Keep an **O**pen mind
Don't seek **P**erfection
Enjoy some **Q**uiet time
Keep your **R**eality in check
Gratitude is a **S**tate of mind
Everything begins with **T**hought
Seek **U**nderstanding
Define your **V**alues
Find meaning in your **W**ork
Avoid e**X**cess
You matter most
Zen

GOLDEN RULES FOR LIVING

Author Unknown

If you open it, close it.

If you turn it on, turn it off.

If you unlock it, lock it up.

If you break it, admit it.

If you can't fix it, call in someone who can.

If you borrow it, return it.

If you value it, take care of it.

If you make a mess, clean it up.

If you move it, put it back.

If it belongs to someone else and you want to use it, get permission.

If you don't know how to operate it, leave it alone.

If it's none of your business, don't ask questions.

If it ain't broke, don't fix it.

If it brightens someone's day, say it.

If it tarnishes someone's reputation, keep it to yourself.

THE SECRET OF LIFE

Author Unknown

As the Lord God was creating the world he called upon his archangels.

The Lord asked his archangels to help him decide where to put the Secret of Life.

"Bury it in the ground," one angel replied.

"Put it on the bottom of the sea," said another.

"Hide it in the mountains," another suggested.

The Lord replied, "If I see to do any of those only a few will find the Secret of Life. The Secret of Life must be accessible to everyone!"

One angel replied, "I know: put it in each man's heart. Nobody will think to look there."

"Yes!" said the Lord. "Within each man's heart."

The Secret of Life lies within all of us.

IT'S UP TO YOU

Author Unknown

One song can spark a moment,
One flower can wake a dream.
One tree can start a forest,
One bird can herald spring.
One smile begins a friendship,
One handclasp lifts a soul.
One star can guide a ship to sea,
One word can frame the goal.
One vote can change a nation,
One sunbeam lights a room.
One candle wipes out darkness,
One laugh will conquer gloom.
One step must start each journey,
One word must start each prayer.
One hope will raise our spirits,
One touch can show you care.
One voice can speak with wisdom,
One heart can know what's true.
One life can make the difference,
You see, it's up to you!

DIRECTIONS FOR LIVING

Author Unknown

The best way to get even is to forget.
Feed your faith and your doubts will starve to death.
God wants spiritual fruit, not religious nuts.
Some folks wear their halos much too tight.
Some marriages are made in heaven...
but they ALL have to be maintained on earth.
Unless you can create the WHOLE universe in 5 days...
then perhaps giving "advice" to God, isn't such a good idea!
Sorrow looks back, worry looks around, and faith looks up.
Standing in the middle of the road is dangerous...
You will get knocked down by the traffic from both ways.
Words are windows to the heart.
A skeptic is a person who...
when he sees the handwriting on the wall claims it's a forgery.
It isn't difficult to make a mountain out of a molehill; just add a little dirt.
A successful marriage isn't finding the right person ...
It's BEING the right person.
The mighty oak tree was once a little nut that held its ground.
Too many people offer God prayers, with claw marks all over them.

The tongue must be heavy indeed, because so few people can hold it
To forgive is to set the prisoner free...
and then discover the prisoner was you.
You have to wonder about humans...
they think God is dead and Elvis is alive!
It's all right to sit on your pity pot every now and again...
Just be sure to flush when you are done.
You'll notice that a turtle only makes progress when it sticks out it's neck.
If the grass is greener on the other side of the fence...
you can bet the water bill is higher.

THE 'SECOND' TEN COMMANDMENTS

Author Unknown

Thou should not worry, for worry is the most unproductive of all human activities.

Thou shall not be fearful, for most of the things we fear never come to pass.

Thou shall not cross bridges before you come to them, for no one yet has succeeded in accomplishing this.

Thou shall face each problem as it comes--you can only handle one at a time anyway.

Thou shall not take problems to bed with you, for they make very poor bedfellows.

Thou shall not borrow other people's problems. They can better care for them than you can.

Thou shall not try to relive yesterday for good or ill, it is forever gone. Concentrate on what is happening in your life and be happy now!

Thou shall be a good listener, for only when you listen do you hear different ideas from your own. It is hard to learn something new when you are talking, and some people do know more than you do.

Thou shall not become "bogged down" by frustration, for 90 percent of it is rooted in self-pity and will only interfere with positive action.

Thou shall count thy blessings, never overlooking the small ones, for a lot of small blessings add up to a big one.

THE TEN "SIGNS" OF LIFE

By RUSS ULMER

YIELD

We all like to be right but sometimes it's better to yield, step aside and let someone else be right.

STOP

A complete and total stop is required here. Re-evaluate the journey while at a stop. Be sure to look both ways before proceeding.

DO NOT ENTER

We all know our limits and there are times that we don't need to "go there".

PRIVATE

It's okay to have those things that only "we" know about.

OPEN / CLOSED

Keep your mind open. We have more clarity when our mind is open as opposed to having it closed.

PLEASE SEAT YOURSELF

Sometimes you just have to do it yourself. In life nothing worthwhile is handed to you, it's earned through hard work and perseverance.

REST AREA

Life is hectic. Our bodies and minds can only take so much. This is a sign that must be obeyed. Enjoy the rest.

REDUCE SPEED AHEAD

When we don't have the time to stop, we must take the time to at least slow down. The present moment only goes at one speed.

ROUGH ROAD AHEAD
This is a sign that we must try to remain aware of. Often we make the mistake of seeing the sign but not proceeding with caution.

EXIT
The final sign in life. Remember an exit from one room is only an entrance into another.

- 2 -
CHILDHOOD

The best thing to spend on your child is your time.
Louise Hart

QUOTES ABOUT CHILDREN

Children are living jewels dropped unsustained from heaven.
Robert Pollok

Babies are such a nice way to start people.
Don Harold

Having children makes one no more a parent than having a piano makes you a pianist.
Michael Levine

Life is a flame that is always burning itself out, but it catches fire again every time a child is born.
George Bernard Shaw

Most of us became parents long before we have stopped being children.
Mignon McLaughlin

Parents are the last people on earth who ought to have children.
Samuel Butler

In automobile terms, the child supplies the power but the parents have to do the steering.
Benjamin Spock

Parents are not quite interested in justice, they are interested in quiet.
Bill Cosby

Your children need your presence more than your presents.
Jesse Jackson

A child is a curly, dimpled lunatic.
Ralph Waldo Emerson

If you bungle raising your children, I don't think whatever else you do well matters very much.
Jacqueline Kennedy Onassis

Children need models rather than critics.
Joseph Joubert

A torn jacket is soon mended; but hard words bruise the heart of a child.
Henry Wadsworth Longfellow

What is done to children, they will do to society.
Karl A. Menninger

Always be nice to your children because they are the ones who will choose your rest home.
Phyllis Diller

Do not train a child to learn by force or harshness; but direct them to it by what amuses their minds, so that you may be better able to discover with accuracy the peculiar bent of the genius of each.
Plato

The best thing to spend on your child is your time.
Louise Hart

Live so that when your children think of fairness and integrity, they think of you.
H. Jackson Brown jr.

Children need guidance and sympathy far more than instruction.
Anne Sullivan

Setting an example is not the main means of influencing another, it is the only means.
Albert Einstein

Children have never been very good at listening to their elders, but they have never failed to imitate them.
James Baldwin

Children are the bridge to heaven.
Persian Proverb

Your children will see what you're all about by what you live rather than what you say.
Dr. Wayne Dyer

Children are unpredictable. You never know what inconsistency they're going to catch you in next.
Franklin P. Jones

The best way to make children good is to make them happy.
Oscar Wilde

Many things can wait; the child cannot. Now is the time his bones are being formed, his mind is being developed. To him, we cannot say tomorrow; his name is today.
Gabriela Mistral

Every child is an artist. The problem is how to remain an artist once he grows up.
Pablo Picasso

You are the bows from which your children, as living arrows, are sent forth.
Kahlil Gibran

We cannot fashion our children after our desires, we must have them and love them as God has given them to us.
Johann Wolfgang Von Goethe

We inevitably doom our children to failure and frustration when we try to set their goals for them.
Dr. Jess Lair

You may give them your love but not your thoughts, for they have their own thoughts. You may house their bodies but not their souls, for their souls dwell in the house of tomorrow, which you cannot visit, not even in your dreams.
Kahlil Gibran

I have found the best way to give advice to your children is to find out what they want and then advise them to do it.
Harry S. Truman

Listen to the desires of your children. Encourage them and then give them the autonomy to make their own decision.
Denis Waitley

By giving children lots of affection, you can help fill them with love and acceptance of themselves. Then that's what they will have to give away.
Dr. Wayne Dyer

The best training any parent can give a child is to train the child to train himself.
P. Gouthey

To endure is the first thing that a child ought to learn, and that which he will have the most need to know.
Jean Jacques Rousseau

Children are apt to live up to what you believe of them.
Lady Bird Johnson

How is it that little children are so intelligent and men so stupid? It must be education that does it.
Alexandre Dumas

THINGS I'VE LEARNED FROM MY CHILDREN

Author Unknown

A king-size waterbed holds enough water to fill a 2000 sq. foot house 4 inches deep.

If you spray hair spray on dust bunnies and run over them with rollerblades, they can ignite.

A 3-year olds voice is louder than 200 adults in a crowded restaurant.

If you hook a dog leash over a ceiling fan, the motor is not strong enough to rotate a 42-pound boy wearing Batman underwear and a Superman cape.

It is strong enough, however, if tied to a paint can, to spread paint on all four walls of a 20 by 20 foot room.

You should not throw baseballs up when the ceiling fan is on.

When using the ceiling fan as a bat, you have to throw the ball up a few times before you get a hit.

A ceiling fan can hit a baseball a long way.

The glass in windows (even double pane) doesn't stop a baseball hit by a ceiling fan.

When you hear the toilet flush and the words "Uh-oh," it's already too late.

Brake fluid mixed with Clorox makes smoke, and lots of it.
A six-year old can start a fire with a flint rock even though a 36-year old man says they can only do it in the movies.

A magnifying glass can start a fire even on an overcast day.

Certain LEGOs will pass through the digestive tract of a four-year old.

Play Dough and Microwave should never be used in the same sentence.

Super glue is forever.

No matter how much Jell-O you put in a swimming pool, you still can't walk on water.

Pool filters do not like Jell-O.

VCR's do not eject PB&J sandwiches even though TV commercials show they do.

Garbage bags do not make good parachutes.

Marbles in gas tanks make lots of noise when driving.

You probably do not want to know what that odor is.

Always look in the oven before you turn it on. Plastic toys do not like ovens.

The fire department in Austin, TX has a 5-minute response time.

The spin cycle on the washing machine does not make earthworms dizzy.

It will, however, make cats dizzy.

PICTURE OF GOD

Author Unknown

A small child was drawing a picture and his teacher said, "That's an interesting picture. Tell me about it."

"It's a picture of God."

"But nobody knows what God looks like."

"They will when I get done."

WHEN YOU THOUGHT I WASN'T LOOKING

Author Unknown

When you thought I wasn't looking, I saw you hang my first painting on the refrigerator, and I wanted to paint another one.

When you thought I wasn't looking, I saw you feed a stray cat, and I thought it was good to be kind to animals.

When you thought I wasn't looking, I saw you make my favorite cake just for me, and I knew that the little things are special things.

When you thought I wasn't looking, I heard you say a prayer, and I believed there is a God I could always talk to.

When you thought I wasn't looking, I felt you kiss me good night, and I felt loved.

When you thought I wasn't looking, I saw tears come from your eyes, and I learned that sometimes things hurt, but it's all right to cry.

When you thought I wasn't looking, I saw that you cared and I wanted to be everything that I could be.

When you thought I wasn't looking, I looked . . . and wanted to say thanks for all the things I saw when you thought I wasn't looking.

LITTLE EYES UPON YOU
AUTHOR UNKNOWN

There are little eyes upon you and they're watching night and day.
There are little ears that quickly take in every word you say.
There are little hands all eager to do anything you do;
And a little boy who's dreaming of the day he'll be like you.

You're the little fellow's idol, you're the wisest of the wise.
In his little mind about you no suspicions ever rise.
He believes in you devoutly, holds all you say and do;
He will say and do, in your way when he's grown up just like you.

There's a wide-eyed little fellow who believes you're always right;
And his eyes are always opened, and he watches day and night.
You are setting an example every day in all you do;
For the little boy who's waiting to grow up to be like you.

THE THINGS CHILDREN SAY

Author Unknown

A mother was driving with her three young children one warm summer evening when a woman in the convertible ahead of us stood up and waved. She was stark naked! As I was reeling from the shock, I heard my 5-year-old shout from the back seat, "Mom! That lady isn't wearing a seat belt!"

On the first day of school, a first grader handed his teacher a note from his mother. The note read, "The opinions expressed by this child are not necessarily those of his parents."

A mother was showing her son how to zip up his coat. "The secret," she said, "is to get the left part of the zipper to fit in the other side before you try to zip it up." The boy looked at her quizzically: "Why does it have to be a secret?"

A little boy got lost at the YMCA and found himself in the women's locker room. When he was spotted, the room burst into shrieks, with ladies grabbing towels and running for cover. The little boy watched in amazement and then asked, "What's the matter -- haven't you ever seen a little boy before?"

WE LOVE OUR KIDS, KINDA

Author Unknown

If you have a lot of tension and you get a headache, do what it says on the aspirin bottle: "Take two aspirin" and "Keep away from children."

You spend the first 2 years of their life teaching them to walk and talk. Then you spend the next 16 telling them to sit down and shut up.

Grandchildren are God's reward for not killing your children.

Cleaning your house while your kids are still growing is like cleaning the driveway before it has stopped snowing.

Mothers of teens know why animals eat their young.

I asked Mom if I was a gifted child ... she said they certainly wouldn't have paid for me.

The main purpose of holding children's parties is to remind yourself that there are children more awful than your own.

We child proofed our home three years ago and they're still getting in!

Be nice to your kids. They'll choose your nursing home.

LAWS OF THE TODDLER

Author Unknown

1. If I like it, it's mine.

2. If it's in my hand, it's mine.

3. If I can take it from you, it's mine.

4. If I had it a little while ago, it's mine.

5. If it's mine, it must never appear to be yours in any way.

6. If I'm doing or building something, all the pieces are mine
.

7. If it looks just like mine, it's mine.

8. If I think it's mine, it's mine.

GREAT TRUTHS ABOUT LIFE THAT LITTLE CHILDREN HAVE LEARNED

Author Unknown

No matter how hard you try, you can't baptize cats.

When your mom is mad at your dad, don't let her brush your hair.

If your sister hits you, don't hit her back. They always catch the second person.

Never ask your 3 -year old brother to hold a tomato.

You can't trust dogs to watch your food.

Reading what people write on desks can teach you a lot.

Don't sneeze when someone is cutting your hair.

Puppies still have bad breath even after -eating a tic tac

Never hold a dust-buster and a cat at the same time.

School lunches stick to the wall.

You can't hide a piece of broccoli in a glass of milk.

Don't wear polka-dot underwear under white shorts.

The best place to be when you are sad is in Grandma's lap.

- 3 -
LEARNING

Thoroughly to teach another is the best way to learn for yourself.
Tryon Adams

QUOTES FOR TEACHERS AND LEARNING

What's done to children, they will do to society.
Karl Menninger

To teach is to learn.
Chinese Proverb

To be a teacher in the right sense is to be a learner.
Kierkegaard

Teaching is the royal road to learning.
Jessamyn West

By learning you will teach; by teaching you will learn.
Latin Proverb

Any man who has been a teacher retains something of a student within him.
Alfred de Vigny

Teachers are expected to reach unattainable goals with inadequate tools. The miracle is that at times they accomplish this impossible task.
Haim G. Ginot

We have lots of heroes today - sportsmen, supermodels, media personalities. They come, they have their 15 minutes of fame, and they go. But the influence of good teachers stays with us. They are the people who really shape our life.
Jonathan Sacks

Teachers don't just teach; they can be vital personalities who help young people to mature, to understand the world and to understand themselves.
Charles Platt

Teachers open our eyes to the world. They give us curiosity and confidence. They teach us to ask questions. They connect us to our past and future. They are the guardians of our social heritage. Life without a teacher is simply not a life.
Jonathan Sacks

A good teacher is one who helps you become who you feel yourself to be. A good teacher is also one who says something you won't understand until ten years later.
Julius Lester

The mediocre teacher tells. The good teacher explains. The superior teacher demonstrates. The great teacher inspires.
William Arthur Ward

It is the supreme art of the teacher to awaken joy in creative expression and knowledge.
Albert Einstein

What is the duty of the teacher if not to inspire?
Bharati Mukherjee

The object of teaching a child is to enable him to get along without a teacher.
Elbert Hubbard

Good teachers are costly, but bad teachers cost more.
Bob Talbert

I touch the future. I teach.
Christa Mcauliffe

To teach is to touch lives forever.
Unknown

To teach is to learn twice.
Joseph Joubert

A teacher who arouses a feeling in us for one good action, one good poem, accomplishes more than the teacher who fills our heads with interminable lists of natural objects.
Goethe

To be fond of learning is to be near to knowledge.
Tze-sze

The classroom – not the trench – is the frontier of freedom now and forevermore.
Lyndon B. Johnson

Education's purpose is to replace an empty mind with an open one.
Malcolm S. Forbes

Next in importance to freedom and justice is popular education, without which neither freedom nor justice can be permanently maintained.
James A. Garfield

MY BROTHER'S BOOTS

Author Unknown

Did you hear about the teacher who was helping one of her kindergarten students put on his boots? He asked for help and she could see why.

With her pulling and him pushing, the boots still didn't want to go on.

When the second boot was on, she had worked up a sweat. She almost whimpered when the little boy said, "Teacher, they're on the wrong feet."

She looked and sure enough, they were. It wasn't any easier pulling the boots off than it was putting them on. She managed to keep her cool as together they worked to get the boots back on -- this time on the right feet.
He then announced, "These aren't my boots."

She bit her tongue rather than get right in his face and scream, "Why didn't you say so?" like she wanted to.

Once again she struggled to help him pull the ill-fitting boots off. He then said, "They're my brother's boots. My Mom made me wear them."
She didn't know if she should laugh or cry. She mustered up the grace and courage she had left to wrestle the boots on his feet again.

She said, "Now, where are your mittens?"

He said, "I stuffed them in the toes of my boots."

TOP 10 REASONS TO BECOME A TEACHER

Author Unknown

10. Might have to work for a living otherwise.

9. Spend leisurely summer in intensive therapy attempting to recover strength for a new year.

8. Attempt to discipline tomorrow's leaders today.

7. Joyfully implement wise policies of marvelous administrators, earning thanks of a grateful nation.

6. Massive funding for classroom supplies.

5. Free apples!

4. Practice pedagogy without fear of arrest.

3. Never a stressful moment.

2. Know all the answers on the test.

1. Big bucks!

GIFTS FOR TEACHER

Author Unknown

On the last day of kindergarten, all the children brought presents for their teacher.

The florist's son handed the teacher a gift. She shook it, held it up and said, "I bet I know what it is - it's some flowers!"
"That's right!" shouted the little boy.

Then the candy store owner's daughter handed the teacher a gift.

She held it up, shook it and said. "I bet I know what it is - it's a box of candy!"

"That's right!" shouted the little girl.

The next gift was from the liquor store owner's son. The teacher held it up and saw that it was leaking. She touched a drop with her finger and tasted it. "Is it wine?" she asked.
"No," the boy answered.

The teacher touched another drop to her tongue. "Is it champagne?" she asked.

"No," the boy answered.

Finally, the teacher said, "I give up. What is it?"

The boy replied, "A puppy!"

NO HOMEWORK EXCUSES

Author Unknown

I lost it fighting this kid who said you weren't the best teacher in the school

I was mugged on the way to school and the mugger took everything I had

Our puppy toilet trained on it

Some aliens from outer space borrowed it so they could study how the human brain worked.

I put it in a safe, but lost the combination

I loaned it to a friend, but he suddenly moved away

Our furnace stopped working and we had to burn it to stop ourselves from freezing

I left it in my shirt and my mother put it in the washing machine

I didn't do it because I didn't want to add to your already heavy workload

My little sister ate it

HOW (NOT) TO SPEAK ENGLISH PROPERLY

Author Unknown

1. Verbs HAS to agree with their subjects.

2. Prepositions are not words to end sentences with.

3. And don't start a sentence with a conjunction.

4. It is wrong to ever split an infinitive.

5. Avoid cliches like the plague. (They're old hat)

6. Also, always avoid annoying alliteration.

7. Be more or less specific.

8. Parenthetical remarks (however relevant) are (usually) unnecessary.

9. Also too, never, ever use repetitive redundancies.

10. No sentence fragments.

11. Contractions aren't necessary and shouldn't be used.

12. Foreign words and phrases are not apropos.

13. Do not be redundant; do not use more words than necessary; it's highly superfluous.

14. One should NEVER generalize.

15. Comparisons are as bad as cliches.

16. Eschew ampersands & abbreviations, etc.
17. One-word sentences? Eliminate.

18. Analogies in writing are like feathers on a snake.

19. The passive voice is to be ignored.

20. Eliminate commas, that are, not necessary. Parenthetical words however should be enclosed in commas.

21. Never use a big word when a diminutive one would suffice.

22. Use words correctly, irregardless of how others use them.

23. Understatement is always the absolute best way to put forth earth-shaking ideas.

24. Eliminate quotations. As Ralph Waldo Emerson said, "I hate quotations. Tell me what you know."

25. If you've heard it once, you've heard it a thousand times: Resist hyperbole; not one writer in a million can use it correctly.

26. Puns are for children, not groan readers.

27. Go around the barn at high noon to avoid colloquialisms.

28. Even IF a mixed metaphor sings, it should be derailed.

29. Exaggeration is a billion times worse than understatement.

And the last one...
30. Proofread carefully to see if you any words out.

HOW A CHILD LEARNS
Author Unknown

If a child lives with criticism,
He learns to condemn.

If a child lives with hostility,
He learns to fight.

If a child lives with ridicule,
He learns to be shy.

If a child lives with shame,
He learns to be guilty.

If a child lives with tolerance,
He learns to be patient.

If a child lives with encouragement,
He learns confidence.

If a child lives with praise,
He learns to appreciate.

If a child lives with fairness,
He learns justice.

If a child lives with security,
He learns to have faith.

If a child lives with approval,
He learns to like himself.

If a child lives with acceptance and friendship,
He learns to find love in the world.

- 4 -
FATHERHOOD

There are 3 stages in a man's life: 'My Daddy can whip your Daddy.' 'Aw, Dad, you don't know anything.' 'My father used to say . . .'.
Dwight McSmith

QUOTES ABOUT FATHERHOOD

The worst misfortune that can happen to an ordinary man is to have an extraordinary father.
O'Malley Austin

The most important thing a father can do for his children is to love their mother.
Henry Ward Beecher

Americans are like a rich father who wishes he knew how to give his son the hardships that made him rich.
Robert Frost

What you have inherited from your father, you must earn over again for yourselves, or it will not be yours.
Johann Wolfgang Von Goethe

To be a successful father there's one absolute rule: when you have a kid, don't look at it for the first two years.
Ernest Hemingway

It is easier for a father to have children than for children to have a real father.
Pope John XXIII

It doesn't matter who my father was; it matters who I remember he was.
Anne Sexton

It is admirable for a man to take his son fishing, but there is a special place in heaven for the father who takes his daughter shopping.
John Sinor

When I was a boy of 14, my father was so ignorant I could hardly stand to have the old man around. But when I got to be 21, I was astonished at how much the old man had learned in seven years.
Mark Twain

A father decided to tell his young son the facts of life and was stumped right away by the boy's first question: 'How many are there?'
Unknown

Education is something you get when your father sends you to college. But it isn't complete until you send your son there.
Unknown

The place of the father in the modern suburban family is a very small one, particularly if he plays golf.
Bertrand Russell

By the time a man realizes that maybe his father was right, he usually has a son who thinks he's wrong.
Charles Wadsworth

The gods visit the sins of the fathers upon the children.
Euripides

Some men just aren't cut out for paternity. Better they should realize it before and not after they become responsible for a son.
Lois Mcmaster Bujold

My father hated radio and could not wait for television to be invented so he could hate that too.
Peter De Vries

TOP TEN THINGS YOU'LL NEVER HEAR A DAD SAY

Author Unknown

10. Well, how 'bout that? I'm lost! Looks like we'll have to stop and ask for directions.

9. You know Pumpkin, now that you're thirteen, you'll be ready for un-chaperoned car dates. Won't that be fun?

8. I noticed that all your friends have a certain hostile attitude. I like that.

7. Here's a credit card and the keys to my new car. GO CRAZY!!

6. What do you mean you wanna play football? Figure skating's not good enough for you, son?

5. Your Mother and I are going away for the weekend. You might want to consider throwing a party.

4. Well, I don't know what's wrong with your car. Probably one of those do-hickey thingies--ya know--that makes it run or something. Just have it towed to a mechanic and pay whatever he asks.

3. No son of mine is going to live under this roof without an earring. Now quit your belly-aching, and let's go to the mall.

2. Whaddya wanna go and get a job for? I make plenty of money for you to spend. Here's $100.

1. What do I want for Father's day? Aahh -- don't worry about that. It's no big deal. (Okay, he might say it, but he doesn't mean it!)

THINGS YOU'LL NEVER HEAR FROM MEN

Author Unknown

Here honey, you use the remote.

Ooh, Antonio Banderas AND Brad Pitt? That's one movie I gotta see!

While I'm up, can I get you anything? (well, maybe once)

Aww, forget Monday Night football, let's watch Desperate Housewives.

Hey, let me hold your purse while you try that on.

We never talk anymore.

HOW MUCH DO YOU EARN?

Author Unknown

A man came home from work late again, tired and irritated, to find his 5-year-old son waiting for him at the door.
"Daddy, may I ask you a question?"
"Yeah, sure, what is it?" replied the man.
"Daddy, how much money do you make an hour?"
"That's none of your business! What makes you ask such a thing?" the man said angrily. "I just want to know. Please tell me, how much do you make an hour?" pleaded the little boy.

"If you must know, I make $20.00 an hour."
"Oh, " the little boy replied, head bowed. Looking up, he asked, "Daddy, may I borrow $10.00, please?"

The father was furious. " If the only reason you want to know how much money I make is just so you can borrow some to buy a silly toy or some other nonsense, then you march yourself straight to your room and go to bed. Think about why you're being so selfish. I work long, hard hours everyday and don't have time for such children's games."

The little boy quietly went to his room and shut the door.
The man sat down and started to get even madder about the little boy's questioning. How dare he ask such questions only to get some money. After an hour or so, the man had calmed down and started to think he may have been a little hard on his son. Maybe there was something he really needed to buy with that $10.00 and he really didn't ask for money very often.
The man went to the door of the little boy's room and opened the door. "Are you asleep son?" he asked.

"No daddy, I'm awake," replied the boy.
"I've been thinking, maybe I was too hard on you earlier," said the man.

"It's been a long day, and I took my aggravation out on you. Here's that $10.00 you asked for."

The little boy sat straight up, beaming. "Oh, thank you daddy!" he yelled.
Then, reaching under his pillow, he pulled out some more crumpled up bills. The man, seeing that the boy already had money, started to get angry again. The little boy slowly counted out his money, then looked up at the man.

"Why did you want more money if you already had some?" the father grumbled.
"Because I didn't have enough, but now I do," the little boy replied. "Daddy, I have a whole $20.00 now. Can I buy an hour of your time?"

AAA DAD

Author Unknown

For 52 years my father got up every morning at 5:30 a.m., except Sunday, and went to work. For 52 years he returned home at 5:30 p.m., like clockwork, for dinner at 6:00 p.m. I never remember my father taking a "night out with the boys," nor do I ever recall my father drinking. All he asked from me as his daughter was to hold his hammer while he repaired something, just so we could have some time to talk to each other.

I never saw my father home from work ill, nor did I ever see my father lay down to take a nap. He had no hobbies, other than taking care of his family.

For 22 years, since I left home for college, my father called me every Sunday at 9:00 a.m. He was always interested in my life, how my family was doing, and I never once heard him lament about his lot in life. The calls even came when he and my mother were in Australia, England or Florida.

Nine years ago when I purchased my first house, my father, 67 years old, spent eight hours a day for three days in the 80-degree Kansas heat, painting my house. He would not allow me to pay someone to have it done. All he asked, was a glass of iced tea, and that a hold a paint brush for him and talk to him. But I was too busy, I had a law practice to run, and I could not take the time to hold the paint brush, or talk to my father.

Five years ago, at age 71 again in the sweltering Kansas heat, my father spent five hours putting together a swingset for my daughter. Again, all he asked was that I get him a glass of iced tea, and talk to him. But again, I had laundry to do, and the house to clean.

Four years ago, my father drove all the way from Denver to Topeka, with an eight foot Colorado Blue Spruce in his trunk, so that my husband and I could have a part of Colorado growing on our land. I was preparing for a trip that weekend and couldn't spend much time tallied to Daddy.

The morning or Sunday, January 16, 1996, my father telephoned me as usual, this time from my sister's home in Florida. We conversed about the tree he had brought me, "Fat Albert," but that morning he called the tree "Fat Oscar," and he had seemed to have forgotten some things we had discussed the previous week. I had to get to church, and I cut the conversation short.

The call came at 4:40 p.m., that day, my father was in the hospital in Florida with an aneurysm. I got on an airplane immediately, and on the way, I thought of all the times I had not taken the time to talk to my father. I realized that I had no idea who he was or what his deepest thoughts were. I vowed that when I arrived, I would make up for the lost time, and have a nice long talk with him and really get to know him.

I arrived in Florida at 1 a.m., my father had passed away at 9:12 p.m. This time it was he who did not have time to talk, or time to wait for me.

In the years since his death I have learned much about my father, and even more about myself. As a father he never asked me for anything but my time, now he has all my attention, every single day.

SOMEBODY SPECIAL

Author Unknown

A teenage boy lived alone with his father. The two of them had a very special relationship. Even though the son was always "warming the bench," his father was always in the stands cheering. He never missed a football game.

This young man was still the smallest of the class when he entered high school.
But his father continued to encourage him but also made it very clear that he did not have to play football if he didn't want to. But the young man loved football and decided to hang in there.

The son was determined to try his best at every practice, and perhaps he'd get to play when he became a senior.

All through high school he never missed a practice but still remained a bench warmer all four years. His faithful father always in the stands, always with words of encouragement for him.

When the young man went to college, he decided to try out for the football team as a "walk-on." Everyone was sure he could never make the cut, but he did. The coach admitted that he kept him on the roster because he always puts his heart and soul to every practice and, at the same time, provided the other members with the spirit and hustle they badly needed.

The news that he had survived the cut thrilled him so much that he rushed to the nearest phone and called his father. His father shared his excitement and was sent season tickets for all the college games.

This persistent young athlete never missed practice during his four years at college, but he never got to play in the game. It was the end of his senior football season, and as he trotted onto the practice field shortly before the big play-off game, the coach met him with a telegram.

The young man read the telegram and he became deathly silent. Swallowing hard, he mumbled to the coach, "My father died this morning. Is it all right if I miss practice today?" The coach put his arm gently around his shoulder and said, "Take the rest of the week off, son. And don't even plan to come back to the game on Saturday."

Saturday arrived, and the game was not going well. In the third quarter, when the team was ten points behind, a silent young man quietly slipped into the empty locker room and put on his football gear. As he ran onto the sidelines, the coach and his players were astounded to see their faithful teammate back so soon.

"Coach, please let me play. I've just got to play today," said the young man. The coach pretended not to hear him. There was no way he wanted his worst player in this close playoff game. But the young man persisted, and finally feeling sorry for the kid, the coach gave in.

"All right," he said, "you can go in." Before long, the coach, the players and everyone in the stands could not believe their eyes. This little unknown, who had never played before was doing everything right.

The opposing team could not stop him. He ran, he passed, blocked and tackled like a star. His team began to triumph. The score was soon tied.
In the closing seconds of the game, this kid intercepted a pass and ran all the way for the winning touchdown!

The fans broke loose. His teammates hoisted him onto their shoulders. Such cheering you've never heard!

Finally, after the stands had emptied and the team had showered and left the locker room, the coach noticed that the young man was sitting quietly in the corner all alone. The coach came to him and said, "Kid, I can't believe it. You were fantastic! Tell me what got into you? How did you do it?"

He looked at the coach, with tears in his eyes, and said, "Well, you knew my dad died, but did you know that my dad was blind?"

The young man swallowed hard and forced a smile, "Dad came to all my games, but today was the first time he could see me play, and I wanted to show him I could do it!"

So remember:
somebody is very proud of you.
somebody is thinking of you.
somebody is caring about you.
somebody misses you.
somebody wants to talk to you.
somebody wants to be with you.
somebody hopes you are not in trouble.
somebody is thankful for the support you have provided.
somebody wants to hold your hand.
somebody hopes everything turns out all right for you.
somebody wants you to be happy.
somebody want you to find him/her.
somebody wants to give you a gift.
somebody wants to hug you.
somebody thinks you ARE a gift.
somebody admires your strength.
somebody wants to protect you.
somebody can't wait to see you.
somebody loves you for who you are.
somebody treasures your spirit.
somebody is glad that you are their friend.
somebody wants to get to know you better.
somebody wants to be near you.
somebody wants you to know they are there for you.
somebody would do anything for you.
somebody wants to share their dreams with you.

somebody is alive because of you.
somebody needs your support.
somebody will cry when they read this.
somebody needs you to have faith in them.
somebody trusts you.
somebody hears a song that reminds them of you.
somebody needs you to send this to them, too.

"To the whole world you might be just one person, but to one person you might be the whole world."

THAT'S MY CHILD

Author Unknown

I was watching some little kids play soccer. These kids were only five or six years old. They were playing a real game - a serious game. Two teams, complete with coaches, uniforms, and parents. I didn't know any of them, so I was able to enjoy the game without the distraction of being anxious about winning or losing. I wished the parents and coaches could have done the same.

The teams were pretty evenly matched. I will just call them Team One and Team Two. Nobody scored in the first period. The kids were hilarious. They were clumsy and terribly inefficient. They fell over their own feet, they stumbled over the ball, they kicked at the ball and missed it, but they didn't seem to care. They were having fun.

In the second quarter, the Team One coach pulled out what must have been his first team and put in the scrubs, except for his best player who now guarded the goal. The game took a dramatic turn. I guess winning is important even when you're five years old, because the Team Two coach left his best players in, and the Team One scrubs were no match for them.

Team Two swarmed around the little guy who was now the Team One goalie. He was an outstanding athlete, but he was no match for three or four who were also very good. Team Two began to score. The Team One goalie gave it everything he had, recklessly throwing his body in front of incoming balls, trying valiantly to stop them.

Team Two scored two goals in quick succession. It infuriated the young boy. He became a raging maniac - shouting, running, diving. With all the stamina he could muster, he covered the boy who now had the ball, but that boy kicked it to another boy twenty feet away, and by the time he repositioned himself, it was too late - Team Two scored a third goal.

I soon learned who the goalie's parents were. They were nice, neat-looking people. I could tell that his dad had just come from the office - he still had his suit and tie on. They yelled encouragement to their son. I became totally absorbed, watching the boy on the field and his parents on the sidelines. After the third goal, the little kid changed. He could see it was no use, he couldn't stop them. He didn't quit, but he became quite desperate, futility was written all over him. His father changed, too. He had been urging his son to try harder, yelling advice and encouragement.

But then he changed. He became anxious. He tried to say that it was okay - to hang in there. He grieved for the pain his son was feeling. After the fourth goal, I knew what was going to happen. I've seen it before.

The little boy needed help so badly, and there was no help to be had. He retrieved the ball from the net and handed it to the referee and then he cried. He just stood there while huge tears rolled down both cheeks. He went to his knees and put his fists to his eyes - and he cried the tears of the helpless and brokenhearted.

When the boy went to his knees, I saw the father start onto the field. His wife clutched his arm and said, "Jim, don't. You'll embarrass him." But he tore loose from her and ran onto the field. He wasn't supposed to -- the game was still in progress. Suit, tie, dress shoes and all, he charged onto the field, and he picked up his son so everybody would know that this was his boy, and he hugged him and held him and cried with him. I've never been so proud of a man in my life. He carried him off the field, and when he got close to the sidelines I heard him say, "Scotty, I'm so proud of you. You were great out there. I want everybody to know that you are my son."

"Daddy," the boy sobbed, "I couldn't stop them. I tried, Daddy, I tried and tried, and they scored on me."

"Scotty, it doesn't matter how many times they scored on you. You're my son, and I'm proud of you. I want you to go back out there and finish the game.

I know you want to quit, but you can't. And, son, you're going to get scored on again, but it doesn't matter. Go on now"

It made a difference - I could tell it did. When you're all alone and you're getting scored on - and you can't stop them, it means a lot to know that it doesn't matter to those who love you. The little guy ran back on to the field-and they scored two more times, but it was okay.

THE FATHER'S GIFT

Author Unknown

A young man was getting ready to graduate from college. For many months he had admired a beautiful sports car in a dealer's showroom, and knowing his father could well afford it, he told him that was all he wanted.

As Graduation Day approached, the young man awaited signs that his father had purchased the car. Finally, on the morning of his graduation, his father called him into his private study. His father told him how proud he was to have such a fine son and told him how much he loved him. He handed his son a beautifully wrapped gift box.

Curious, and somewhat disappointed, the young man opened the box and found a lovely, leather-bound Bible, with the young man's name embossed in gold. Angry, he rose his voice to his father and said, "with all your money, you give me a Bible?" and stormed out of the house.

Many years passed and the young man was very successful in business. He had a beautiful home and wonderful family, but realized his father was very old, and thought perhaps he should go to him. He had not seen him since that graduation day.

Before he could make arrangements, he received a telegram telling him his father had passed away and willed all of his possessions to his son. He needed to come home immediately and take care of things.

When he arrived at his father's house, sudden sadness and regret filled his heart. He began to search through his father's important papers and saw the still gift-wrapped Bible, just as he had left it years ago. With tears, he opened the Bible and began to turn the pages. His father had carefully underlined a verse, Matt.7:11, "And if ye, being evil, know how to give good gifts to your children, how much more shall your Heavenly Father which is in Heaven, give to those who ask Him?"

As he read those words, a car key dropped from the back of the Bible. It had a tag with the dealer's name, the same dealer who had the sports car he had desired. On the tag was the date of his graduation, and the words PAID IN FULL.

How many times do we miss God's blessings because we can't see past our own desires?

THE GOLDEN BOX

Author Unknown

Some time ago a friend of mine punished his 3-year-old daughter for wasting a roll of gold wrapping paper. Money was tight, and he became infuriated when the child tried to decorate a box to put it under their Christmas tree.

Nevertheless, the little girl brought the gift to her father the next morning and said, "This is for you daddy." He was embarrassed by his earlier overreaction, but his anger flared again when he found that the box was empty.

He yelled at her, "Don't you know that when you give someone a present, there's supposed to be something inside of it?"

The little girl looked up at him with tears in her eyes and said, "Oh daddy, it's not empty. I blew kisses into the box. All for you Daddy."

The father was crushed. He put his arms around his little girl and again begged her forgiveness.

My friend told me that he kept that gold box by his bed for years. Whenever he was discouraged, he would take out an imaginary kiss and remember the love of the child who had put it there.

In a very real sense, each of us as parents has been given a gold container filled with unconditional love and kisses from our children. No more precious possession could anyone hold.

THE MAN IN THE GLASS

Author Unknown

When you get what you want in your struggle for self,
And the world makes you King for a Day,
Just go to the mirror and look at yourself,
and see what the man has to say.

For it isn't your father or mother,
Whose judgment upon you must pass,
The fellow whose verdict counts most in your life,
Is the one staring back from the glass.

You may fool the whole world down the pathway of years,
And get pats on the back as you pass,
But your final reward will be heartache and tears,
If you've cheated the man in the glass.

He's the fellow to please, never mind all the rest,
for he's with you clear to the end,
And you've passed your most dangerous test,
If the man in the glass is your friend.

WHAT IS A FATHER?

Author Unknown

A father is a person who is forced to endure childbirth without an anesthetic. He growls when he feels good and laughs very loud when he is scared half-to-death.

A father never feels entirely worthy of the worship in a child's eyes. He is never quite the hero his daughter thinks. Never quite the man his son believes him to be. And this worries him sometimes. (So he works too hard to try to smooth the rough places in the road of those of his own who will follow him.)

A father is a person who goes to war sometimes ... and would run the other way except that war is part of his only important job in his life, (which is making the world better for his child than it has been for him).

Fathers grow older faster than people, because they, in other wars, have to stand at the train station and wave goodbye to the uniform that climbs on board.

And, while mothers cry where it shows, fathers stand and beam -- outside -- and die inside.

Fathers are men who give daughters away to other men, who aren't nearly good enough, so that they can have children that are smarter than anybody's.

Fathers fight dragons almost daily. They hurry away from the breakfast table, off to the arena which is sometimes called an office or a workshop. There, with callused hands, they tackle the dragon with three heads: Weariness, Works, and Monotony. And they never quite win the fight, but they never give up.

Knights in shining armor; fathers in shiny trousers. There's little difference as they march away each workday.

I don't know where father goes when he dies, but I've an idea that, after a good rest, wherever it is, he won't just sit on a cloud and wait for the girl he's loved and the children she bore. He'll be busy there too -- repairing the stars, oiling the gates, improving the streets, smoothing the way.

- 5 -
MOTHERHOOD

Who takes the child by the hand takes the mother by the heart.
German Proverb

QUOTES ON MOTHERHOOD

A mother is she who can take the place of all others but whose place no one else can take.
Cardinal Mermillod

Motherhood is a wonderful thing - what a pity to waste it on children.
Judith Pugh

....my opinion is that the future good or bad conduct of a child depends on its mother.
Letizia Ramolino Buonaparte, Napoleon's mother

Mothers are the pivot on which the family spins,
Mothers are the pivot on which the world spins.
Pam Brown

A mother is not a person to lean on, but a person to make learning unnecessary.
Dorothy Canfield Fisher

It will be gone before you know it. The fingerprints on the wall appear higher and higher. Then suddenly they disappear.
Dorothy Evslin

Cleaning your house while your kids are still growing is like shoveling the walk before it stops snowing.
Phyllis Diller

Any mother could perform the jobs of several air-traffic controllers with ease.
Lisa Alther

All that I am, or hope to be, I owe to my angel mother.
Abraham Lincoln

Mother -- that was the bank where we deposited our hurts and worries.
Dewitt Talmage

God could not be everywhere, so he created mothers.
Jewish Proverb

Sooner or later we all quote our mothers.
Bern Williams

The most remarkable thing about my mother is that for thirty years she served the family nothing but leftovers. The original meal has never been found.
Calvin Trillin

My mother had a great deal of trouble with me, but I think she enjoyed it.
Mark Twain

Most turkeys taste better the day after my mother's tasted better the day before.
Rita Rudner

Neurotics build castles in the air; psychotics live in them. My mother cleans them.
Rita Rudner

M-O-T-H-E-R

By Howard Johnson

"M" is for the million things she gave me,
"O" means only that she's growing old,
"T" is for the tears she shed to save me,
"H" is for her heart of purest gold;
"E" is for her eyes, with love-light shining,
"R" means right, and right she'll always be,
Put them all together, they spell "MOTHER,"
A word that means the world to me.

SMALL BLESSINGS

Author Unknown

Dear Lord, it's such a hectic day
With little time to stop and pray
For life's been anything but calm
Since You called on me to be a mom
Running errands, matching socks
Building dreams with building blocks
Cooking, cleaning, and finding shoes
And other stuff that children lose
Getting lids on bottled bugs
Wiping tears and giving hugs
A stack of last week's mail to read
So where's the quiet time I need?
Yet when I steal a minute, Lord
Just at the sink or ironing board
To ask the blessings of Your grace
I seen then, in my small one's face
That you have blessed me
All the while
And I stop to kiss
That precious smile

SEIZE THE MOMENT

Author Unknown

Too many people put off something that brings them joy just because they haven't thought about it, don't have it on their schedule, didn't know it was coming or are too rigid to depart from their routine.

I got to thinking one day about all those women on the Titanic who passed up dessert at dinner that fateful night in an effort to cut back. From then on, I've tried to be a little more flexible. How many women out there will eat at home because their husband didn't suggest going out to dinner until after something had been thawed? Does the word "refrigeration" mean nothing to you? How often have your kids dropped in to talk and sat in silence while you watched Jeopardy! On television? I cannot count the times I called my sister and said, "How about going to lunch in a half hour?" She would gasp and stammer, "I can't."

Check one:
"I have clothes on the line."
"My hair is dirty."
"I wish I had known yesterday,"
"I had a late breakfast".
"It looks like rain".

And my personal favorite: "It's Monday". She died a few years ago. We never did have lunch together.

Because Americans cram so much into their lives, we tend to schedule our headaches. We live on a sparse diet of promises we make to ourselves when all the conditions are perfect: We'll go back and visit the Grandparents when we get Stevie toilet trained. We'll entertain, when we replace the living room carpet. We'll go on a second honeymoon, when we get two more kids out of college. Life has a way of accelerating as we get older. The days get shorter, and the list of promises to ourselves gets longer. One morning, we awaken, and all we have to show for our lives is a litany of "I'm going to", "I plan on" and "Someday, when things are settled down a bit."

When anyone calls my 'seize the moment' friend, she is open to adventure and available for trips. She keeps an open mind on new ideas. Her enthusiasm for life is contagious. You talk with her for five minutes, and you're ready to trade your bad feet for a pair of Rollerblades and skip an elevator for a bungee cord. My lips have not touched ice cream in 10 years. I love ice cream. It's just that I might as well apply it directly to my hips with a spatula and eliminate the digestive process. The other day, I stopped the car and bought a double-decker. If my car had hit an iceberg on the way home, I would have died happy.

Now...go on and have a nice day. Do something you WANT to ...not something on your SHOULD DO list.

REAL MOMS

Author Unknown

Real Mothers don't eat quiche; they don't have time to make it.

Real Mothers know that their kitchen utensils are probably in the sandbox.

Real Mothers often have sticky floors, filthy ovens and happy kids.

Real Mothers know that dried play dough doesn't come out of shag carpets.

Real Mothers don't want to know what the vacuum just sucked up.

Real Mothers sometimes ask "why me?" and get their answer when a little voice says, "because I love you best."

Real Mothers know that a child's growth is not measured by height or years or grade. It is marked by the progression of Ma-ma to Mommy to Mom.

BEFORE I WAS A MOM

Author Unknown

Before I was a mom
I made and ate hot meals.
I had unstained clothing.
I had quiet conversations on the phone.
I slept as late as I wanted and never worried about how late I got into bed.
I brushed my hair and my teeth everyday.

Before I was a mom
I cleaned my house each day.
I never tripped over toys or forgot words to lullabies.
I didn't worry whether or not my plants were poisonous.
I never thought about immunizations.

Before I was a mom
I had never been
pooped on
spit on
chewed on
peed on
or pinched by tiny fingers.

Before I was a mom
I had complete control of
my thoughts
my body
and my mind.
I slept all night.

Before I was a mom
I never held down a screaming child
so that doctors could do tests or give shots
I never looked into teary eyes and cried.

I never got gloriously happy over a simple grin.
I never sat up late hours at night watching a baby sleep.

Before I was a mom
I never held a sleeping baby just because I didn't want to put it down.
I never felt my heart break into a million pieces when I couldn't stop the hurt.
I never knew that something so small could affect my life so much.
I never knew that I could love someone so much.
I never knew I would love being a mom.

Before I was a mom
I didn't know the feeling of having my heart outside my body.
I didn't know how special it could feel to feed a hungry baby.
I didn't know that bond between a mother and her child.
I didn't know that something so small could make me feel so important.

Before I was a mom
I had never gotten up in the middle of the night every 10 minutes to make sure all was OK
I had never known the warmth
the joy
the love
the wonderfulment
or the satisfaction of being a mom.
I didn't know I was capable of feeling so much
Before I was a Mom

MY MOTHER TAUGHT ME...

Author Unknown

My mother taught me CONSIDERATION FOR OTHERS....
"I just scrubbed that floor. Go outside and bleed in the entry."

My Mother taught me LOGIC...
"If you fall off that swing and break your neck, you can't go to the store with me."

My Mother taught me MEDICINE...
"If you don't stop crossing your eyes, they're going to freeze that way."

My Mother taught me TO THINK AHEAD...
"If you don't pass your spelling test, you'll never get a good job!"

My Mother taught me ESP...
"Put your sweater on; don't you think that I know when you're cold?"

My Mother taught me TO MEET A CHALLENGE...
"What were you thinking? Answer me when I talk to you...Don't talk back to me!"

My Mother taught me HUMOR...
"When that lawn mower cuts off your toes, don't come running to me."

My Mother taught me how to BECOME AN ADULT...
"If you don't eat your vegetables, you'll never grow up."

My mother taught me ABOUT SEX...
"How do you think you got here?"

My mother taught me about GENETICS...
"You are just like your father!"

My mother taught me about my ROOTS...
"Do you think you were born in a barn?"

My mother taught me about the WISDOM of AGE...
"When you get to be my age, you will understand."

My mother taught me about ANTICIPATION...
"Just wait until your father gets home."

My mother taught me about RECEIVING...
"You are going to get it when we get home."

And my all time favorite thing --- JUSTICE...
"One day you will have kids, and I hope they turn out just like YOU... then you'll see what it's like."

IS HEAVEN IN THE YELLOW PAGES?

Author Unknown

Mommy went to Heaven, but I need her here today.
My tummy hurts & I fell down, I need her right away.
Operator can you tell me how to find her in this book?
Is Heaven in the yellow part, I don't know where to look.

I think my daddy needs her too, at night I hear him cry.
I hear him call her name sometimes, but I really don't know why.
Maybe if I call her, she will hurry home to me.
Is Heaven very far away, is it across the sea?

She's been gone a long, long time she needs to come home now!
I really need to reach her, but I simply don't know how.
Help me find the number please, is it listed under "Heaven"?
I can't read these big, big words, I am only seven.

I'm sorry operator, I didn't mean to make you cry,
Is your tummy hurting too, or is it there something in your eye?
If I call my church maybe they will know.
Mommy said when we need help that's where we should go.

I found the number to my church tacked up on the wall.
Thank you operator, I'll give them a call.

MOM'S DEFINITIONS

Author Unknown

AIRPLANE: What Mom impersonates to get a one-year-old to eat strained beets.

ALIEN: What Mom would suspect had invaded her house if she spotted a child-sized creature cleaning up after itself.

APPLE: Nutritious lunchtime dessert that children will trade for cupcakes.

BABY: 1. Dad, when he gets a cold. 2. Mom's youngest child, even if he's 42.

BATHROOM: A room used by the entire family, believed by all (except Mom) to be self-cleaning.

BECAUSE: Mom's reason for having kids do things that can't be explained logically.

BED & BREAKFAST: Two things the kids will never make for themselves.

CARPET: Expensive floor covering used to catch spills and clean mud off shoes.

CAR POOL: Complicated system of transportation where Mom always winds up going the farthest with the biggest bunch of kids who have had the most sugar.

CHINA: Legendary nation reportedly populated by children who love leftover vegetables.

COOK: 1. Act of preparing food for consumption. 2. Mom's other name.

COUCH POTATO: What Mom finds under the sofa cushions after the kids eat dinner.

DATE: Infrequent outings with Dad where Mom can enjoy worrying about the kids in a different setting.

DRINKING GLASS: Any carton or bottle left open in the fridge.

DUST: Insidious interloping particles of evil that turn a home into a battle zone.

DUST RAGS: See "DAD'S UNDERWEAR."

EAR: A place where kids store dirt.

EAT: What kids do between meals, but not at them.

EMPTY NEST: See"WISHFUL THINKING."

ENERGY: Element of vitality kids always have an oversupply of until asked to do something.

"EXCUSE ME": One of Mom's favorite phrases, reportedly used in past times by children.

EYE: The highly susceptible optic nerve that, according to Mom, can be "put out" by anything from a suction-arrow to a carelessly handled butter knife.

FABLE: A story told by a teenager arriving home after curfew.

FOOD: The response Mom usually gives in answer to the question "What's for dinner tonight?" See "SARCASM."

FROZEN: 1. A type of food. 2. How hell will be when Mom lets her daughter date an older guy with a motorcycle.

GARBAGE: A collection of refuse items, the taking out of which Mom assigns to a different family member each week, then winds up doing herself.

GENIUSES: Amazingly, all of Mom's kids.

GUM: Adhesive for the hair and carpet.

HAMPER: A wicker container with a lid, usually surrounded by, but not containing, dirty clothing.

HANDI-WIPES: Pants, shirt-sleeves, drapes, etc.

HANDS: Body appendages that must be scrubbed raw with volcanic soap and sterilized in boiling water immediately prior to consumption of the evening meal.

HINDSIGHT: What Mom experiences from changing too many diapers.

HOMEMADE BREAD: An object of fiction like the Fountain of Youth and the Golden Fleece.
ICE: Cubes of frozen water that would be found in small plastic tray if kids or husbands ever filled the darn things instead of putting them back in the freezer empty.

INSIDE: That place that will suddenly look attractive to kids once Mom has spent a minimum of half an hour getting them ready to go outside.

"I SAID SO": Reason enough, according to Mom.

JACKPOT: When all the kids stay at friends' homes for the night.

JEANS: According to kids, appropriate for just about any occasion, including church and funerals.

"JEEEEEEEEZ!": Slang for "Gee, Mom, isn't there anything else you can do to embarrass me in front of my friends?"

JOY RIDE: Going somewhere without the kids.

JUNK: Dad's stuff.

KETCHUP: The sea of tomato-based goop kids use to drown the dish that Mom spent hours cooking and years perfecting to get the seasoning just right.

KISS: Mom medicine.

LAKE: Large body of water into which a kid will jump should his friends do so.

LEMONADE STAND: Complicated business venture where Mom buys powdered mix, sugar, lemons, and paper cups, and sets up a table, chairs, pitchers, and ice for kids who sit there for three to six minutes and net a profit of 15 cents.

LIE: An "exaggeration" Mom uses to transform her child's papier-mache volcano science project into a Nobel Prize-winning experiment and a full-ride scholarship to Harvard.

LOSERS: See "Kids' Friends."

- 6 -
FRIENDSHIP

The only to way to have a friend is to be one.
Ralph Waldo Emerson

QUOTES ON FRIENDSHIP

True friendship comes when silence between two people is comfortable.
Dave Tyson Gentry

A friend is someone who knows all about you and loves you just the same.
Elbert Hubbard

It is not the talking that counts between friends, it is the never needing to say what counts.
Shawn Green

Friendship improves happiness, and abates misery, by doubling our joy, and dividing our grief.
Joseph Addison

The best way to keep your friends is not to give them away.
Wilson Mizner

The best time to make friends is before you need them.
Ethel Barrymore

A friend is someone who allows you distance but is never far away.
Noah Benshea

A true friend is someone who is there for you when he'd rather be anywhere else.
Len Wein

The essence of true friendship is to make allowances for another's little lapses.
David Storey

True friendship is seen through the heart not through the eyes.
Anonymous

A friend costs nothing. An enemy you must pay for.
Yiddish Folk Saying

A faithful friend is the medicine of life.
Ecclesiastes 6:16

True friendship is like sound health, the value of it is seldom known until it be lost.
Charles Caleb Colton

Life's truest happiness is found in friendships we make along the way.
Anonymous

The happiest in all the world
Is that of making friends,
And no investment on the street
Pays larger dividends,
For life is more than stocks and bonds,
And love than rate percent,
And he who gives in friendship's name
Shall reap what he has spent.
Anonymous

WHAT KIND OF FRIEND ARE YOU?

Author Unknown

A man and his dog were walking along a road. The man was enjoying the scenery, when it suddenly occurred to him that he was dead. He remembered dying, and that the dog had been dead for years. He wondered where the road was leading them.

After a while, they came to a high, white stone wall along one side of the road. It looked like fine marble. At the top of a long hill, it was broken by a tall arch that glowed in the sunlight. When he was standing before it, he saw a magnificent gate in the arch that looked like mother of pearl, and the street that led to the gate looked like pure gold.

He and the dog walked toward the gate, and as he got closer, he saw a man at a desk to one side. When he was close enough, he called out, "Excuse me, where are we?"

"This is Heaven, sir," the man answered.
"Wow! Would you happen to have some water?" the man asked.
"Of course, sir. Come right in, and I'll have some ice water brought right up." The man gestured, and the gate began to open.
"Can my friend," gesturing toward his dog, "come in, too?" the traveler asked.
"I'm sorry, sir, but we don't accept pets."
The man thought a moment and then turned back toward the road and continued the way he had been going.
After another long walk, and at the top of another long hill, he came to a dirt road which led through a farm gate that looked as if it had never been closed. There was no fence.
As he approached the gate, he saw a man inside, leaning against a tree and reading a book.
"Excuse me!" he called to the reader. "Do you have any water?"
"Yeah, sure, there's a pump over there" The man pointed to a place that couldn't be seen from outside the gate. "Come on in."
"How about my friend here?" the traveler gestured to the dog.

"There should be a bowl by the pump."

They went through the gate, and sure enough, there was an old-fashioned hand pump with a bowl beside it. The traveler filled the bowl and took a long drink himself, then he gave some to the dog. When they were full, he and the dog walked back toward the man who was standing by the tree waiting for them.
"What do you call this place?" the traveler asked.
"This is Heaven," was the answer.
"Well, that's confusing," the traveler said. "The man down the road said that was Heaven, too."
"Oh, you mean the place with the gold street and pearly gates? Nope. That's Hell."
"Doesn't it make you mad for them to use your name like that?"
"No. I can see how you might think so, but we're just happy that they screen out the folks who'll leave their best friends behind.

FRIENDSHIP

By MARCUS BROWN

Friendship is something that lasts a lifetime
Whether you're his friend or whether you're mine
Though all of us may not look alike
Friends stick together even after a fight
A friend is there for you when the rope gets short
And you should be there for them when they need support
A real friend does not down another
They treat them like a sister or brother
Friendship is you
Friendship is me

A FRIEND...

Author Unknown

(A)ccepts you as you are
(B)elieves in "you"
(C)alls you just to say "HI"
(D)oesn't give up on you
(E)nvisions the whole of you (even the unfinished parts)
(F)orgives your mistakes
(G)ives unconditionally
(H)elps you
(I)nvites you over
(J)ust "be" with you
(K)eeps you close at heart
(L)oves you for who you are
(M)akes a difference in your life
(N)ever Judges
(O)ffer support
(P)icks you up
(Q)uiets your fears
(R)aises your spirits
(S)ays nice things about you
(T)ells you the truth when you need to hear it
(U)nderstands you
(V)alues you
(W)alks beside you
(X)-plains thing you don't understand
(Y)ells when you won't listen and
(Z)aps you back to reality

TRUE FRIEND

Author Unknown

A girl asked a guy if he thought she was pretty,
He said...no.

She asked him if he would want to be with her forever....
and he said no.

She then asked him if she were to leave would he cry,
and once again he replied with a no.

She had heard enough. As she walked away, tears streaming down her face.

The boy grabbed her arm and said....

You're not pretty, you're beautiful.

I don't want to be with you forever, I NEED to be with you forever.

And I wouldn't cry if you walked away...I'd die...

Remember:
"A good friend will not come bail you out of jail....But a true friend will be sitting next to you saying ....WE screwed up!

FLOWERS NEED SUNSHINE
THOUGHTS ON FRIENDSHIP
Author Unknown

☺ Flowers need sunshine, violets need dew, all angels in heaven know I need u. years may fly, tears may dry, but my friendship with u will never die.

☺ One day you will ask me: What is more important to you, me or your life? I will say: my life… You will walk away from me without knowing that YOU ARE MY LIFE!!!

☺ Feel good when somebody Miss You. Feel better when somebody loves you. But feel best when somebody never forgets you.

☺ A friend is sweet when it's new….but it is sweeter when it's TRUE! But you know what? It's sweetest when it's you.

☺ A friend gives hope when life is low, a friend is a place when you have nowhere to go, a friend is honest, and a friend is true. A friend is precious a friend is you.

☺ If kisses were water, I will give you a sea. If hugs were leaves, I will give you a tree. If you love a planet, I will give u a galaxy; if friendship is life I will give you mine.

☺ People live People die People Laugh People Cry Some give up Some will try Some say hi Some say bye Others may forget YOU but never will I.

☺ If I were to be anything in this world…. I'd be your tears!!!… So, I can be conceived in your heart, born in your eyes, live on your cheeks & die on your lips!!!!!

- ☺ If you are a chocolate you're the sweetest, if you are a Teddy Bear you're the most huggable, if you are a Star you're the Brightest, and since you are my "FRIEND" you're the "BEST"!!!!!!!!!

- ☺ A special friend is rare indeed, it beams to be special breed. Yes, perfect friends are very few, so lucky I'm for having you.

- ☺ Time might lead me to nowhere and faith might break into pieces but I will always be THANKFUL that once in my life's journey we became FRIENDS!

- ☺ It takes half our life to find true friends & half of it keeping them. I am lucky to have spent less than half my life finding you & wish to spend the rest keeping you.

- ☺ A memory lasts forever, and never does it die. True friends stay together and never say good bye.

- ☺ Always draw a circle around the ones you love, never draw a heart because hearts can be broken, but circles are never ending.

- ☺ Of all the gifts, big and small, your friendship is the greatest of them all.

- ☺ The morning is just a few moments away. Go to sleep and when you wake up, remember me as a friend who is always there for you and never let you down

- ☺ If you are in trouble, if you need a hand, just call my number, because I'm your friend!

- ☺ Whenever I see your smiling face, I have to smile myself, because I like you, you're my friend!!!

☺ You cannot buy friendship, you can earn it. If someone comes for help, be a true friend!

☺ A friend is always welcome ... Early in the morning or late at night. Time is of no importance ... When it concerns real friendship!!

☺ Friendship is a wonderful word; it might be the most beautiful one on earth. Friendship is something powerful, a gift of great value!

☺ No gold or precious stones ... give us happiness and peace, friendship and its warmth ... will bring it to us.

☺ There is a big difference between friendship and a rose... Roses last only a while ... but friendship is forever

☺ Friends are like stars... you don't see them all the time, but you know they're there!

☺ Life is not easy and it will never be, but you've got friends and one of them is me.

☺ I must have been born under a lucky star, to find a friend as nice as you are. I will follow the rainbow to the end, if you promise to remain my friend!!!

☺ When friendship is deeply rooted, it is a plant that cannot even be uprooted by a storm....

☺ A friend is someone who knows when you need her...

☺ A friend is someone who knows the song of your heart and who can sing it for you when you have forgotten it

☺ Friend: someone who tells you things while you are alive, things that others tell after you die

- ☺ You can eat and drink together, talk and laugh together, enjoy life together, but you are only real friends when you also cried together.

A GIFT FROM GOD

Author Unknown

One day, when I was a freshman in high school, I saw a kid from my class was walking home from school. His name was Kyle. It looked like he was carrying all of his books. I thought to myself, "Why would anyone bring home all his books on a Friday? He must really be a nerd."

I had quite a weekend planned (parties and a football game with my friends tomorrow afternoon), so I shrugged my shoulders and went on.

As I was walking, I saw a bunch of kids running toward him. They ran at him, knocking all his books out of his arms and tripping him so he landed in the dirt. His glasses went flying, and I saw them land in the grass about ten feet from him. He looked up and I saw this terrible sadness in his eyes. My heart went out to him. So, I jogged over to him and as he crawled around looking for his glasses, and I saw a tear in his eye.

As I handed him his glasses, I said, "Those guys are jerks. They really should get lives."

He looked at me and said, "Hey thanks!" There was a big smile on his face.

It was one of those smiles that showed real gratitude. I helped him pick up his books, and asked him where he lived. As it turned out, he lived near me, so I asked him why I had never seen him before. He said he had gone to private school before now. I would have never hung out with a private school kid before.
We talked all the way home, and I carried his books. He turned out to be a pretty cool kid. I asked him if he wanted to play football on Saturday with me and my friends. He said yes.

We hung all weekend and the more I got to know Kyle, the more I liked him. And my friends thought the same of him. Monday morning came, and there was Kyle with the huge stack of books again. I stopped him and said, "Darn boy, you are gonna really build some serious muscles with this pile of books everyday!" He just laughed and handed me half the books.

Over the next four years, Kyle and I became best friends. When we were seniors, we began to think about college. Kyle decided on Georgetown, and I was going to Duke. I knew that we would always be friends, that the miles would never be a problem. He was going to be a doctor, and I was going for business on a football scholarship.

Kyle was valedictorian of our class. I teased him all the time about being a nerd. He had to prepare a speech for graduation. I was so glad it wasn't me having to get up there and speak.

Graduation day, I saw Kyle. He looked great. He was one of those guys that really found himself during high school. He filled out and actually looked good in glasses. He had more dates than me and all the girls loved him!

Boy, sometimes I was jealous. Today was one of those days. I could see that he was nervous about his speech. So, I smacked him on the back and said, "Hey, big guy, you'll be great!" He looked at me with one of those looks (the really grateful one) and smiled. "Thanks," he said.

As he started his speech, he cleared his throat, and began. "Graduation is a time to thank those who helped you make it through those tough years. Your parents, your teachers, your siblings, maybe a coach ... , but mostly your friends. I am here to tell all of you that being a friend to someone is the best gift you can give them. I am going to tell you a story."

I just looked at my friend with disbelief as he told the story of the first day we met. He had planned to kill himself over the weekend. He talked of how he had cleaned out his locker so his mom wouldn't have to do it later and was carrying his stuff home. He looked hard at me and gave me a little smile. "Thankfully, I was saved. My friend saved me from doing the unspeakable."

I heard the gasp go through the crowd as this handsome, popular boy told us all about his weakest moment. I saw his mom and dad looking at me and smiling that same grateful smile. Not until that moment did I realize its depth.

Never underestimate the power of your actions. With one small gesture you can change a person's life. For better or for worse. God puts us all in each other's lives to impact one another in some way. Look for God in others.

Each day is a gift from God! Don't forget to say, "Thank you!"

IDEAS OF A FRIEND

Author Unknown

In first grade your idea of a good friend was the person who went to the bathroom with you and held your hand as you walked through the scary hall.

In second grade your idea of a good friend was the person who helped you stand up to the class bully.

In third grade your idea of a good friend was the person who shared their lunch with you when you forgot yours on the bus.

In fourth grade your idea of a good friend was the person who was willing to switch square dancing partners in gym so you wouldn't have to be stuck do-si-do-ing with Nasty Nick or Smelly Susan.

In fifth grade your idea of a friend was the person who saved a seat on the back of the bus for you.

In sixth grade your idea of a friend was the person who went up to Nick or Susan, your new crush, and asked them to dance with you, so that if they said no you wouldn't have to be embarrassed.

In seventh grade your idea of a friend was the person who let you copy the Math homework from the night before that you had.

In eighth grade your idea of a good friend was the person who helped you pack up your stuffed animals and old baseball but didn't laugh at you when you finished and broke out into tears.

In ninth grade your idea of a good friend was the person who would go to a party thrown by a senior so you wouldn't wind up being the only freshman there.

In tenth grade your idea of a good friend was the person who changed their schedule so you would have someone to sit with at lunch.

In eleventh grade your idea of a good friend was the person who gave you rides in their new car, convinced your parents that you shouldn't be grounded, consoled you when you broke up with Nick [or Glenn] or Susan, and found you a date to the prom.

In twelfth grade your idea of a good friend was the person who helped you pick out a college /university, assured you that you would get into that college/university, helped you deal with your parents who were having a hard time adjusting to the idea of letting you go...

At graduation your idea of a good friend was the person who was crying on the inside but managed the biggest smile one could give as they congratulated you.

The summer after twelfth grade your idea of a good friend was the person who helped you clean up the bottles from that party, helped you sneak out of the house when you just couldn't deal with your parents, assured you that now that you and Nick or you and Susan were back together, you could make it through anything, helped you pack up for university and just silently hugged you as you looked through blurry eyes at 18 years of memories you ere leaving behind, and finally on those last days of childhood, went out of their way to give you reassurance that you would make it in college as well as you had these past 18 years, and most importantly sent you off to college knowing you were loved.

Now, your idea of a good friend is still the person who gives you the better of the two choices, holds your hand when you're scared, helps you fight off those who try to take advantage of you, thinks of you at times when you are not there, reminds you of what you have forgotten, helps you put the past behind you but understands when you need to hold on to it a little longer, stays with you so that you have confidence, goes out of their way to make time for you, helps you clear up your mistakes, helps you deal with pressure from others, smiles for you when they are sad, helps you become a better person, and most importantly loves you!

- 7 -
LOVE & HAPPINESS

Love is the master key which opens the gates of happiness.
Oliver Wendell Holmes, Sr.

QUOTES ABOUT LOVE

One word frees us of all the weight and pain of life: that word is love.
Sophocles

Love is the master key which opens the gates of happiness.
Oliver Wendell Holmes, Sr.

Love … binds everything together in perfect harmony.
Colossians 3:14

The love we give away is the only one we keep.
Elbert Hubbard

If you would be loved, love and be lovable.
Benjamin Franklin

There is only one happiness in life, to love and to be loved.
George Sand

Nine times out of ten, when you extend your arms to someone, they will step in, because basically they need precisely what you need.
Leo Buscaglia

Thou shalt love thy neighbor as thyself.
Leviticus 19:18

If you judge people, you have no time to love them.
Mother Teresa

The essence of love is kindness.
Robert Louis Stevenson

Love is, above all, the gift of oneself.
Jean Anouilh

A five-word sentence that could change the world tomorrow is "What would love do now?"
Neale Donald Walsch

Do not seek perfection in a changing world. Instead, perfect your love.
Master Sengstan

The supreme happiness in life is the conviction that we are loved.
Victor Hugo

Love is not just caring deeply, it's, above all understanding.
Francoise Sagan

Love is an irresistible desire to be irresistibly desired.
Robert Frost

To love deeply in one direction makes us more loving in all others.
Anne-Sophie Swetchine

Nothing takes the taste out of peanut butter quite like unrequited love.
Charles M. Schulz, Charlie Brown in "Peanuts"

There is no remedy for love but to love more.
Henry David Thoreau

Love is the difficult realization that something other than oneself is real.
Iris Murdoch

Age does not protect you from love. But love, to some extent, protects you from age.
Jeanne Moreau

To love is to receive a glimpse of heaven.
Karen Sunde

Love is an act of endless forgiveness, a tender look which becomes a habit.
Peter Ustinov

Love is not blind - it sees more, not less. But because it sees more, it is willing to see less.
Rabbi Julius Gordon

It is better to have loved and lost than never to have lost at all.
Samuel Butler

WESTMINSTER ABBEY

Author Unknown

The following words were discovered on the tomb of an Anglican Bishop (1100 A. D.) in the Crypts of Westminster Abbey:

When I was young and free and my imagination had no limits, I dreamed of changing the world. As I grew older and wiser, I discovered the world would not change, so I shortened my sights somewhat and decided to change only my country.

But it, too, seemed immovable.

As I grew into my twilight, in one last desperate attempt, I settled for changing only my family, those closest to me, but alas, they would have none of it.

And now as I lie on my deathbed, I suddenly realize: If I had only changed myself first, then by example I would have changed my family.

From their inspiration and encouragement, I would then have been able to better my country and who knows, I may have even changed the world.

LOVE IS A WONDERFUL WORD

Author Unknown

Love is a wonderful word. It's the kind of word that makes you feel warm and tingly inside. Sometimes love is all you need.

We all go through a stage in our life where you love someone and they don't love you back and you're hurt; you're very hurt and you feel like you just want to die because you cannot be with that person or just even to be close to them. The hardest thing is to see them love someone else. But try to think back when you didn't even know that person or you even hated that person.

Love is a great feeling, right? You will feel this way again; maybe not now, maybe not later, but soon. After all the hurt is gone, you will love again and even stronger than before.

Remember, there are so many guys in this world. Don't let one get you down because it's not worth it and obviously they're not worth your time.

Love truly is a wonderful word, especially when you both share it. You will find someone; just hold on and don't give up.

YOU KNOW

Author Unknown

You know you're in love when you can say anything to the person and you know they won't laugh at you.

When you can see their face when you close your eyes.
When you can still feel their arms around you holding you tight long after they are gone.
When you can still taste their kiss after you have said good-bye.

You can tell you're in love when you miss them before they are gone.

When their voice lingers in your ears.
When their presence eases any pain.
When their name sends chills down your spine.
When they are the only thing you can think about.

You know you're in love when you can see all their hopes and dreams and their soul when you look into their eyes.

When they call you at four in the morning and say, "I love you" and mean it.
When your tears stain not only their shirt, but also their heart.
When they are hurt just because of these tears.
When even a simple chore done with them can become a lasting memory.

Ultimately, you know you're in love when you can't imagine living without them, and can't figure, how did you live before you knew them.

When they fulfill every need and without them you are incomplete.

The love of someone else completes the heart, and soul, and mind all at once.

QUOTES ON HAPPINESS

Now and then it's good to pause in our pursuit of happiness and just be happy.
Guillaume Apollinaire

Happiness is a perfume which you cannot pour on someone without getting some on yourself.
Ralph Waldo Emerson

The pursuit of happiness is a most ridiculous phrase; if you pursue happiness you'll never find it.
Charles Percy Snow

Happiness is a how, not a what; a talent, not an object.
Hermann Hesse

I, not events, have the power to make me happy or unhappy today. I can choose which it shall be. Yesterday is dead, tomorrow hasn't arrived yet. I have just one day, today, and I'm going to be happy in it.
Groucho Marx

The place to be happy is here, the time to be happy is now.
Robert Ingersoll

If only we'd stop trying to be happy we could have a pretty good time.
Edith Wharton

Very little is needed to make a happy life; it is all within yourself, in your way of thinking.
Marcus Aurelius

Many people think that if they were only in some other place, or had some other job, they would be happy. Well, that is doubtful. So get as much happiness out of what you are doing as you can and don't put off being happy until some future date.
Dale Carnegie

No man is happy without a delusion of some kind. Delusions are as necessary to our happiness as realities.
Christian Nevell Bovee

Dedicate yourself to the good you deserve and desire for yourself. Give yourself peace of mind. You deserve to be happy. You deserve delight.
Mark Victor Hansen

The secret of happiness is to make others believe they are the cause of it.
Al Batt

Happiness is nothing more than good health and a bad memory.
Albert Schweitzer

The happiness of a man in this life does not consist in the absence but in the mastery of his passions.
Alfred Lord Tennyson

Happiness is that state of consciousness which proceeds from the achievement of one's values.
Ayn Rand

If there were in the world today any large number of people who desired their own happiness more than they desired the unhappiness of others, we could have paradise in a few years.
Bertrand Russell

Cherish all your happy moments: they make a fine cushion for old age.
Christopher Morley

Man is the artificer of his own happiness.
Henry David Thoreau

If we cannot live so as to be happy, let us least live so as to deserve it.
Immanuel Hermann Fichte

The foolish man seeks happiness in the distance, the wise grows it under his feet.
James Oppenheim

Seek not happiness too greedily, and be not fearful of happiness.
Lao-tsze

No man is happy who does not think himself so.
Publilius Syrus

Depend not on another, but lean instead on thyself...True happiness is born of self-reliance.
The Laws of Manu

WHAT HAPPINESS IS

Author Unknown

We convince ourselves that life will be better after we get married, have a baby, then another. Then we are frustrated that the kids aren't old enough and we'll be more content when they are. After that we're frustrated that we have teenagers to deal with. We will certainly be happy when they are out of that stage. We tell ourselves that our life will be complete when our spouse gets his or her act together, when we get a nicer car, are able to go on a nice vacation, when we retire.

The truth is, there's no better time to be happy than right now.
If not now, when?

Your life will always be filled with challenges. It's best to admit this to yourself and decide to be happy anyway. One of my favorite quotes comes from Alfred D Souza. He said, *"For a long time it had seemed to me that life was about to begin - real life. But there was always some obstacle in the way, something to be gotten through first, some unfinished business, time still to be served, a debt to be paid. Then life would begin. At last it dawned on me that these obstacles were my life".*

This perspective has helped me to see that there is no way to happiness.

Happiness is the way. So, treasure every moment that you have. And treasure it more because you shared it with someone special, special enough to spend your time and remember that time waits for no one.

So stop waiting until you finish school, until you go back to school, until you lose ten pounds, until you gain ten pounds, until you have kids, until your kids leave the house, until you start work, until you retire, until you get married, until you get divorced, until Friday night, until Sunday morning, until you get a new car or home, until home is paid off, until spring, until summer, until fall, until winter, until you are off welfare, until the first or fifteenth, until your song comes on, until you've had a drink, until you've sobered up, until you die, until you are born again to decide that there is no better time than right now to be happy.

Happiness is a journey, not a destination. Work like you don't need money, Love like you've never been hurt, And dance like no one's watching.

DESIRE

Author Unknown

An emperor was coming out of his palace for his morning walk when he met a beggar. He asked the beggar, "What do you want?" The beggar laughed and said, "You are asking me as though you can fulfill my desire!"
The king was offended. He said, "Of course I can fulfill your desire. What is it? Just tell me."
And the beggar said, "Think twice before you promise anything."

The beggar was no ordinary beggar, he was the emperors past life master. He had promised in that life, "I will come and try to wake you in your next life. This life you have missed but I will come again." But the king had forgotten completely -- who remembers past lives? So he insisted, "I will fulfill anything you ask. I am a very powerful emperor, what can you possibly desire that I can not give to you?"
The beggar said, "It is a very simple desire. You see this begging bowl? Can you fill it with something?"

The emperor said, "Of course!" He called one of his viziers and told him, "Fill this mans begging bowl with money." The vizier went and got some money and poured it into the bowl, and it disappeared. And he poured more and more,
and the moment he would pour it, it would disappear. And the begging bowl remained always empty.

The whole palace gathered. By and by the rumor went throughout the whole capital, and a huge crowd gathered. The prestige of the emperor was at stake. He said to his viziers, "If the whole kingdom is lost, I am ready to lose it, but I cannot be defeated by this beggar."

Diamonds and pearls and emeralds, his treasuries were becoming empty. The begging bowl seemed to be bottomless. Everything that was put into it -- everything! -- immediately disappeared, went out of existence. Finally it was the evening, and the people were standing there in utter silence. The king dropped at the feet of the beggar and admitted his defeat. He said, "Just tell me one thing. You are victorious - but before you leave, just fulfill my curiosity. What is the begging bowl made of?"

The beggar laughed and said, "It is made up of the human mind. There is no secret. It is simple made up of human desire."

This understanding transforms life. Go into one desire -- what is the mechanism of it? First there is a great excitement, great thrill, adventure. you feel a great kick. Something is going to happen, you are on the verge of it. And then you have the car, you have the yacht, you have the house, you have the woman, and suddenly all is meaningless again.
What happens? Your mind has dematerialized it. The car is standing in the drive, but there is no excitement anymore. The excitement was only in getting it. You became so drunk with the desire than you forgot your inner nothingness. Now the desire is fulfilled, the car in the drive, the woman in your bed, the money in your bank account - again excitement disappears. Again the emptiness is there, ready to eat you up. Again you have to create another desire to escape this yawning abyss.

That's how one moves from one desire to another desire. That's how one remains a beggar. Your whole life proves it again and again -- every desire frustrates. And when the goal is achieved, you will need another desire.
The day you understand that desire as such is going to fail comes the turning point in your life.

The other journey is inwards. move inwards, come back home.

TWO DAY WE SHOULD NOT WORRY

Author Unknown

There are two days in every week about which we should not worry,
two days which should be kept free from fear and apprehension.
One of these days is Yesterday with all its mistakes and cares,
its faults and blunders, its aches and pains.
Yesterday has passed forever beyond our control.
All the money in the world cannot bring back Yesterday.
We cannot undo a single act we performed;
we cannot erase a single word we said.
Yesterday is gone forever.
The other day we should not worry about is Tomorrow
with all its possible adversities, its burdens,
its large promise and its poor performance;
Tomorrow is also beyond our immediate control.
Tomorrow's sun will rise,
either in splendor or behind a mask of clouds, but it will rise.
Until it does, we have no stake in Tomorrow,
for it is yet to be born.
This leaves only one day, Today.
Any person can fight the battle of just one day.
It is when you and I add the burdens of those two awful eternities.
Yesterday and Tomorrow that we break down.
It is not the experience of Today that drives a person mad,
it is the remorse or bitterness of something which happened
Yesterday and the dread of what Tomorrow may bring.
Let us, therefore, Live but **one day at a time**.

- 8 -
WORK & SUCCESS

I never worked a day in my life. It's not work when you love what you're doing.
David Shakarian

QUOTES ABOUT WORK

Success is not the key to happiness. Happiness is the key to success. If you love what you are doing, you will be successful.
Albert Schweitzer

People are always good company when they are doing what they really enjoy.
Samuel Butler

Chose a job you love, and you will never have to work a day in your life.
Confucius

Every calling is great when greatly pursued
Oliver Wendell Holmes

To fulfill a dream, to be allowed to sweat over lonely labor, to be given a chance to create, is the meat and potatoes of life. The money is the gravy.
Bette Davis

The best work never was and never will be done for money.
John Ruskin

I never did a day's work in my life. It was all fun.
Thomas A. Edison

My father always told me, "Find a job you love and you'll never have to work a day in your life."
Jim Fox

When work is a pleasure, life is joy! When work is a duty, life is slavery.
Maxim Gorky

Nothing is work unless you'd rather be doing something else.
George Halas

Get happiness out of your work or you may never know what happiness is.
Elbert Hubbard

When you cease to make a contribution, you begin to die.
Eleanor Roosevelt

If you want creative workers, give them enough time to play.
John Cleese

Pleasure in the job put perfection in the work.
Aristotle

Real success is finding your lifework in the work that you love.
David McCullough

Getting fired is nature's way to telling you that you had the wrong job in the first place.
Hal Lancaster

People forget how fast you did a job - but they remember how well you did it.
Howard Newton

Nothing is really work unless you would rather be doing something else.
James M. Barrie

Plans are only good intentions unless they immediately degenerate into hard work.
Peter Drucker

Hard work spotlights the character of people: some turn up their sleeves, some turn up their noses, and some don't turn up at all.
Sam Ewing

It's not the hours you put in your work that counts, it's the work you put in the hours.
Sam Ewing

Far and away the best prize that life offers is the chance to work hard at work worth doing.
Theodore Roosevelt

I'm a great believer in luck, and I find the harder I work the more I have of it.
Thomas Jefferson

Whoever does not love his work cannot hope that it will please others.
Unknown

OCCUPATIONAL DESCRIPTIONS

Author Unknown

An accountant is someone who knows the cost of everything and the value of nothing.

A banker is a fellow who lends you his umbrella when the sun is shining and wants it back the minute it begins to rain. (Mark Twain)

An economist is an expert who will know tomorrow why the things he predicted yesterday didn't happen today.

A statistician is someone who is good with numbers but lacks the personality to be an accountant.

A programmer is someone who solves a problem you didn't know you had in a way you don't understand.

A lawyer is a person who writes a 10,000 word document and calls it a "brief."

A psychologist is a man who watches everyone else when a beautiful girl enters the room.

A professor is one who talks in someone else's sleep.

A schoolteacher is a disillusioned person who used to think they liked children.

A consultant is someone who takes the watch off your wrist and tells you the time.

THAT'S NOT MY JOB

Author Unknown

This is a story about four people: Everybody, Somebody, Anybody and Nobody.

There was an important job to be done, and Everybody was sure that Somebody would do it. Anybody could have done it but Nobody did it. Somebody got angry about that, because it was Everybody's job. Everybody thought Anybody could do it but Nobody realized that Everybody wouldn't do it.

It ended up that Everybody blamed Somebody when Nobody did what Anybody had done.

QUOTES ON SUCCESS

Success is not the key to happiness. Happiness is the key to success. If you love what you are doing, you will be successful.
Albert Schweitzer

Success is nothing more than a few simple disciplines, practiced every day.
Jim Rohn

There are no secrets to success. It is the result of preparation, hard work, learning from failure.
Colin Powell

Success seems to be connected with action. Successful people keep moving. They make mistakes, but they don't quit.
Conrad Hilton

Eighty percent of success is showing up.
Woody Allen

The secret of success is learning how to use pain and pleasure instead of having pain and pleasure use you. If you do that, you're in control of your life. If you don't, life controls you.
Anthony Robbins

It is literally true that you can succeed best and quickest by helping others to succeed.
Napoleon Hill

It's simply a matter of doing what you do best and not worrying about what the other fellow is going to do.
John R. Amos

If you want to be successful, find someone who has achieved the results you want and copy what they do and you'll achieve the same results.
Anthony Robbins

Employ your time in improving yourself by other men's writings so that you shall come easily by what others have labored hard for.
Socrates

No one lives long enough to learn everything they need to learn starting from scratch. To be successful, we absolutely, positively have to find people who have already paid the price to learn the things that we need to learn to achieve our goals.
Brian Tracy

People of mediocre ability sometimes achieve outstanding success because they don't know when to quit. Most men succeed because they are determined to.
George E. Allen

Do what you can, with what you have, where you are.
Theodore Roosevelt

It is a mistake to look too far ahead. Only one link in the chain of destiny can be handled at a time.
Winston Churchill

ELEMENTS OF SUCCESS FROM A TO Z

By RUSS ULMER

Attitude is everything
Be willing to take a risk
Change is constant
Don't burn bridges
Education and training
Find a mentor
Give back what you receive
Honor your commitments
If you don't do it, someone else will
Just do it
Keep a Focus
Listen
Maintain a balance
Never lose sight of your goals
Overcome your fears
Peer rapport is important
Quiet your mind
Remain dedicated to your dream
Seize opportunities
Think big
Understand your intuition
Visualize
What does success mean to you?
e**X**tra hard work won't kill you
Your best is all you can do
Zest for life

TO HAVE SUCCEEDED
BY RALPH WALDO EMERSON

To laugh often and love much;
To win the respect of intelligent people
And win the affection of children;
To earn the approbation of honest critics
And endure the betrayal of false friends;
To appreciate beauty;
To find the best in others;
To give one's self;
To leave the world a little better,
Whether by a healthy child,
A garden patch,
Or a redeemed social condition;
To have played and laughed with enthusiasm
And sung with exultation;
To know even one life has breathed easier
Because you have lived . . .
This is to have succeeded.

BEN FRANKLIN'S
13 PRINCIPLES OF SUCCESS

In the year 1723, a seventeen-year-old boy arrived in Philadelphia without a penny to his name. At age 42, he retired, wealthy. Few men, before or since have ever been as successful as Benjamin Franklin. He gave credit for his many inventions and business successes to this list of 13 principles. Each of them should be practiced in order, for a week at a time, so that all of them become a habit in your life. They'll work as well today as they did then.

TEMPERANCE: Eat not dullness; drink not to elevation.

SILENCE: Speak not but what may benefit others or yourself, avoid trifling conversation.

ORDER: Let all your things have their place; let each part of your business have it's time.

RESOLUTION: Resolve to perform what you ought; perform without fail what you resolve.

FRUGALITY: Make no expense but to do good to others or yourself; waste nothing.

INDUSTRY: Lose no time; be always employed in something useful; cut off all unnecessary actions.

SINCERITY: Use no harmful deceit; think innocently and justly; and if you speak, speak accordingly.

JUSTICE: wrong none by doing injuries or omitting the benefits that are your duty.

MODERATION: Avoid extremes; forebear resenting injuries so much as you think they deserve.

CLEANLINESS: Tolerate no uncleanness in body, clothes or habitation.

TRANQUILITY: Be not disturbed at trifles, nor at accidents.

CHASTITY: Be chaste in matters with the opposite sex.

HUMILITY: Imitate Jesus and Socrates.

KEEP SWIMMING

Author Unknown

Two frogs fell into a deep cream bowl.
One was an optimistic soul.
But the other took the gloomy view.
"We'll drown," he lamented without much ado,
and with a last despairing cry,
he flung up his legs and said "Goodbye."

Quote the other frog with a steadfast grin,
"I can't get out but I won't give in,
I'll just swim around till my strength is spent,
then I'll die the more content."
Bravely he swam to work his scheme,
and his struggles began to churn the cream.

The more he swam, his legs a flutter,
the more the cream turned into butter.
On top of the butter at last he stopped,
and out of the bowl he gaily hopped.

What is the moral? It's easily found...
If you can't hop out, keep swimming around!

LESSONS OF FAILURE

Author Unknown

Lord, are you trying to tell me something?
For...

Failure does not mean I'm a failure;
It does mean I have not yet succeeded.

Failure does not mean I have accomplished nothing;
It does mean I have learned something.

Failure does not mean I have been a fool;
It does mean I had enough faith to experiment.

Failure does not mean I have disgraced;
It does mean I have dared to try.

Failure does not mean I don't have it;
It does mean I have something to do in a different way.

Failure does not mean I am inferior;
It does mean I am not perfect.

Failure does not mean I have wasted my life;
It does mean that I have an excuse to start over.

Failure does not mean that I should give up;
It does mean that I should try harder.

Failure does not mean that I will never make it;
It does mean that I need more practice.

Failure does not mean that you have abandoned me;
It does mean that you must have a better idea

- 9 -
STRESS & CHANGE

This, too, shall pass.
William Shakespeare

QUOTES ABOUT STRESS

The chief cause of stress is reality.
Lily Tomlin

No one can escape stress, but you can learn to cope with it. Practice positive thinking…seize control in small ways.
Adele Scheele

Stress – that confusion created when the mind must override the body's basic desire to choke the living #@!&? Out of some idiot who desperately needs it.
Unknown

If I knew what I was so anxious about, I wouldn't be so anxious.
Mignon Mclaughlin

Keep breathing.
Sophie Tucker

If you can't help it, don't think about it.
Carmel Myers

For fast acting relief, try slowing down.
Lily Tomlin

Burnout is all in the mind, primarily the lack of stretching and exciting goals and expectations, fueled by a growing awareness of one's strengths and possibilities.
Joe Batten

50 EASY STRESSBUSTERS
BY RUSS ULMER

Go for a walk ☺
Take a hot bath ☺
Light a scented candle ☺
Wear clothes that fit ☺
Have positive people in your life ☺
Have unplanned days ☺
Let people know what you need ☺
Write in a journal ☺
Laugh once in a while ☺
Keep a positive perspective on your problems ☺
Indulge your inner child ☺
Compliment someone ☺
Do a random act of kindness ☺
Play with a child ☺
Use please and thank you ☺
Have faith in yourself ☺
Say a daily affirmation ☺
Have a vision or focus ☺
Tell someone a joke ☺
Stay in the present moment ☺
Go out dancing ☺
Hug someone ☺
Take a risk ☺
Concentrate on your breathing ☺
Read to a child ☺
Listen to relaxing, quiet music ☺
Decrease or discontinue caffeine ☺
Read a book ☺
Send yourself flowers ☺
Send flowers to a friend ☺
Join a club ☺
Turn off the TV ☺
Practice relaxation techniques ☺
Go for a drive in the country ☺

Don't expect perfection ☺
Get a good night's sleep ☺
Watching a funny movie ☺
Work in the yard or garden ☺
Get a massage ☺
Attend to your spiritual needs ☺
Sing in the car ☺
Volunteer ☺
Send a letter to a friend ☺
Take a nap ☺
Don't gossip ☺
Smile ☺
Do things that make you happy ☺
Develop more patience ☺
Let someone else be right ☺
Help someone you don't know ☺

REMEMBER THAT STRESS IS AN ATTITUDE

REDUCE YOUR STRESS FROM A to Z

BY RUSS ULMER

Assert yourself
Be active
Compliment someone
Don't do more than you can
Enjoy nature
Friends and family
Get organized
Have fun
Indulge your inner child
Just do it
Keep a positive outlook
Learn something new
Make spirituality a part of your life
Nobody's perfect
Open up your mind
Plan time for yourself
Quiet time
Relax
Simplify your life
Take care of your health
Understand that stress is an attitude
Volunteer
Work can be a big source of stress
e**X**tra sleep can be good
You matter most
Zebras don't have stress

QUOTES ON CHANGE

There is no way to make people like change. You can only make them feel less threatened by it.
Frederick Hayes

The new always carries with it the sense of violation, of sacrilege. What is dead is sacred; what is new, that is different, is evil, dangerous, or subversive.
Henry Miller

Even if you're on the right track, you'll get run over if you just sit there.
Will Rogers

All progress has resulted from people who took unpopular positions.
Adlai Stevenson

If you're through changing, you're through
Bruce Barton

The reasonable man adapts himself to the world; the unreasonable one persists in trying to adapt the world to himself. Therefore, all progress depends on the unreasonable man.
George Bernard Shaw

If you realize that all things change, there is nothing you will try to hold onto.
Tao Te Ching

Discoveries are often made by not following instructions, by going off the main road, by trying the untried.
Frank Tyger

The only way to discover the limits of the possible is to go beyond them into the impossible.
Arthur C. Clark

We must choose. Be a child of the past with all its crudities and imperfections, its failures and defeats, or a child of the future, the future of symmetry and ultimate success.
Frances E. Willard

If you can't change your fate, change your attitude.
Amy Tan

It's the most unhappy people who most fear change.
Mignon Mclaughlin

If you fear change, leave it here.
Sign on a restaurant tip jar

They always say time changes things, but you actually have to change them yourself.
Andy Warhol

Only I can change my life. No one can do it for me.
Carol Burnett

Change is the constant, the signal for rebirth, the egg of the phoenix.
Christina Baldwin

Nothing endures but change.
Heraclitus

It's not that some people have willpower and some don't. It's that some people are ready to change and others are not.
James Gordon, M.D.

We did not change as we grew older; we just became more clearly ourselves.
Lynn Hal

The universe is change; our life is what our thoughts make it.
Marcus Aurelius Antoninus

FIVE SHORT CHAPTERS ON CHANGE

Author Unknown

Chapter 1.
I walk down a street and there's a deep hole in the sidewalk. I fall in. It takes forever to get out. It's my fault.

Chapter 2.
I walk down the same street. I fall in the hole again. It still takes a long time to get out. It's not my fault.

Chapter 3.
I walk down the same street. I fall in the hole again. It's becoming a habit. It is my fault. I get out immediately.

Chapter 4.
I walk down the same street and see the deep hole in the sidewalk. I walk around it.

Chapter 5.
I walk down a different street.

THE STARFISH

Author Unknown

One day there was a wise man who used to go to the ocean to do his writing. He had a habit of walking on the beach before he began his work. One day he was walking along the shore. As he looked down the beach, he saw a human figure moving like a dancer. He smiled to himself to think of someone who would dance to the day. So he began to walk faster to catch up. As he got closer, he saw that it was a young man and the young man wasn't dancing, but instead he was reaching down to the shore, picking up something and very gently throwing it into the ocean.

As he got closer he called out, "Good morning! What are you doing?"
The young man paused, looked up and replied, "Throwing starfish into the ocean."

"I guess I should have asked, why are you throwing starfish in the ocean?"
"The sun is up, and the tide is going out, and if I don't throw them in they'll die."

"But, young man, don't you realize that there are miles and miles of beach, and starfish all along it. You can't possibly make a difference!"

The young man listened politely, then bent down, picked up another starfish and threw it into the sea, past the breaking waves and said, "It made a difference for that one."

- 10 -
SPIRITUALITY

Here on earth, God's work must surely be our own.
John F. Kennedy

QUOTES ABOUT RELIGION

People have a peculiar pleasure in making converts, that is, in causing others to enjoy what they enjoy, thus finding their own likeness represented and reflected back to them.
Johann Wolfgang Von Goethe

We must select the illusion which appeals to our temperament, and embrace it with passion, if we want to be happy.
Cyril Connolly

People do more from custom than from reason.
Unknown

People often grudge others what they cannot enjoy themselves.
Aesop

That which we call sin in others, is experiment for us.
Emerson

The demagogue is one who preaches doctrines he knows to be untrue to men he knows to be idiots.
H. L. Mencken

Moral indignation is jealousy with a halo.
H. G. Wells

Most people have seen worse things in private than they pretend to be shocked at in public.
Edgar Watson Howe

Most men would kill the truth if truth would kill their religion.
Lemuel K. Washburn

You can cite a hundred references to show that the biblical God is a bloodthirsty tyrant, but if they can dig up two or three verses that say "God is love" they will claim that you are taking things out of context!
Dan Barker

We must respect the other fellow's religion, but only in the sense and to the extent that we respect his theory that his wife is beautiful and his children smart.
H.l. Mencken

This would be the best of all possible worlds, if there were no religions in it.
John Adams

If 50 million people believe a foolish thing, it is still a foolish thing.
Anatole France

Duration is not a test of truth or falsehood.
Anne Morrow Lindbergh

To judge from the notions expounded by theologians, one must conclude that God created most men simply with a view to crowding hell.
Marquis de Sade

The man who says to me, "Believe as I do, or God will damn you," will presently say, "Believe as I do, or I shall assassinate you."
Voltaire

To rule by fettering the mind through fear of punishment in another world is just as base as to use force.
Hypatia

The difference between a saint and a hypocrite is that one lies for his religion, the other by it.
Minna Antrim

Don't join the book burners. Do not think you are going to conceal thoughts by concealing evidence that they ever existed.
Dwight D. Eisenhower

I cannot conceive of a personal God who would directly influence the actions of individuals, or would directly sit in judgment on creatures of his own creation.
Albert Einstein

How many legs does a dog have if you call the tail a leg? Four. Calling a tail a leg doesn't make it a leg.
Abraham Lincoln

The best way to know God is to love many things.
Vincent van Gogh

THE WISDOM OF BUDDHA

Ambition is like love, impatient both of delays and rivals.

Better than a thousand hollow words, is one word that brings peace.

Consider others as yourself.

Do not dwell in the past, do not dream of the future, concentrate the mind on the present moment.

Every human being is the author of his own health or disease.

An insincere Friend is more to be feared than a wild beast; a wild beast may wound your body, but an evil friend will wound your mind.

Our deeds, Good or evil, follow us like shadows.

Hatred does not cease by hatred, but only by love; this is the eternal rule.

I never see what has been done; I only see what remains to be done.

Just as a candle cannot burn without fire, men cannot live without a spiritual life.

To Keep the body in good health is a duty; other wise the mind is not strong and clear.

Look within, thou art the Buddha

The Mind is the source of happiness and unhappiness.
Neither fire nor wind, birth nor death can erase our good deeds.

Do not Overrate what you have received, nor envy others. He who envies others does not obtain peace of mind.

Peace comes from within. Do not seek it without.

With the Relinquishing of all thought and egoism, the enlightened one is liberated not clinging.

Attachment is the Source of all suffering

Teach this triple truth to all: A generous heart, kind speech, and a life of service and compassion

Unity can only be manifested by the Binary. Unity itself and the idea of Unity are already two.

Virtue is persecuted more by the wicked than it is loved by the good.

We are what we think. All that we are arises with our thoughts. With our thoughts, we make the world.

Your work is to discover your work and then with all your heart give yourself to it.

THE WISDOM OF JESUS

Ask and you shall receive

Bless those who curse you

Condemn not and you will not be condemned

Do good to those who hate you

Fortunate are you who are poor, for yours is the realm of God.

Give and there will be gifts for you

Happy are you who are hungry now, you shall be satisfied

I am the light of the world

Judge not and you will not be judged

Knock and the door will be opened for you

Love your enemies

Happy are the merciful, for they shall be shown mercy

Pray for those who treat you badly

Search and you will find

The kingdom of God is among you

When someone strikes you on the right cheek, offer them the other cheek, too.

GETTING INTO HEAVEN

Author Unknown

You can't fool the kids in Sunday school; they are way too smart... "If I sold my house and my car, had a big garage sale, and gave all my money to the church, would I get into heaven?" I asked the children in my Sunday school class.

"NO!" all the children answered.

"If I cleaned the church every day, mowed the yard, and kept everything neat and tidy, would I get into heaven?"

Again the answer was, "NO!"

"Well," I continued, "then how can I get to heaven?"
A five-year-old boy shouted, "You gotta be dead!"

A MEMO FROM GOD

Author Unknown

Date: TODAY
To: YOU
From: THE BOSS
Subject: YOURSELF
Reference: LIFE

I am God. Today I will be handling all of your problems. Please remember that I do not need your help.
If life happens to deliver a situation to you that you cannot handle, do not attempt to resolve it. Kindly put it in the SFGTD (something for God to do) box. All situations will be resolved, but in My time, not yours.
Once the matter is placed into the box, do not hold onto it by worrying about it. Instead, focus on all the wonderful things that are present in your life now.
If you find yourself stuck in traffic, don't despair. There are people in this world for which driving is an unheard of privilege.
Should you have a bad day at work, think of the man who has been out of work for years.
Should you despair over a relationship gone bad, think of the person who has never known what it's like to love and be loved in return.

Should you grieve the passing of another weekend, think of the woman in dire straits, working twelve hours a day, seven days a week to feed her children.
Should your car break down, leaving you miles away from assistance, think of the paraplegic who would love the opportunity to take that walk.
Should you notice a new gray hair in the mirror, think of the cancer patient in chemo who wishes she had hair to examine.
Should you find yourself at a loss and pondering what is life all about, asking what is my purpose? Be thankful. There are those who didn't live long enough to get the opportunity.

Should you find yourself the victim of other people's bitterness, ignorance, smallness or insecurities, remember, things could be worse. You could be one of them!
Should you decide to send this to a friend, thank you, you may have touched their life in ways you will never know!

- 11 -
GROWING OLDER

Everyone is the age of their heart.
Guatemalen Saying

QUOTES ABOUT GROWING OLDER

Age is not important unless you're a cheese.
Helen Hayes

The secret of staying young is to live honestly, eat slowly, and lie about your age.
Lucille Ball

Life begins at forty.
Walter B. Pitkin

I'm over the hill, but the climb was terrific!
Unknown

Just remember, once you're over the hill, you begin to pick up speed.
Charles Schulz

The trick is growing up without growing old.
Casey Stengel

You can't help getting older, but you don't have to get old.
George Burns

Everyone is the age of their heart.
Guatemalan Saying

Middle age is when your age starts to show around your middle.
Bob Hope

Anyone can get old. All you have to do is live long enough.
Groucho Marx

Don't complain about growing old – many people don't have that privilege.
Earl Warren

How old would you be if you didn't know how old you are?
Satchell Paige

AGING GUIDELINES

Author Unknown

You know your getting older when…

Everything hurts and what doesn't hurt, doesn't work.
The gleam in your eye is from the sun hitting your bifocals.
You get winded playing cards.
You look forward to a dull evening.
Your back goes out more often than you do.
Dialing long distance wears you out.
You wear slip-ons because lace-ups wear you out.
Your children are beginning to look old.
Your definition of middle age increases each year.
You long for the days when you took afternoon naps.

AGING PRAYER

Author Unknown

God keep my heart attuned to laughter
When youth is done;

When all the days are gray days, coming after
The warmth, the sun.

God keep me then from bitterness, from grieving,
When life seems cold;

God keep me always loving and believing
As I grow old.

GROWING OLDER

Author Unknown

Lord, thou knowest better than I know myself that I am growing older and will someday be old. Keep me from getting talkative, and particularly from the fatal habit of thinking I must say something on every subject.

Release me from the craving to straighten out everybody else's affairs. Make me thoughtful, but not moody; helpful, but not bossy. With my vast store of wisdom it seems a pity not to use it all – but thou knowest Lord, that I want a few friends at the end.

Keep, my mind free from the recital of endless details; give me wings to get to the point. Seal my lips on my many aches and pains, they are increasing and my love of rehearsing them is becoming greater as the years go by. Teach me the glorious lesson that occasionally it is possible that I may be mistaken.

Keep me reasonably sweet; I do not want to be a saint – some of them are hard to live with – but a sour old man or woman is one of the crowning works of the devil. Help me to extract all possible fun out of life. There are so many funny things around us, and I don't want to miss any of them.

YOU KNOW YOU'RE NO LONGER A KID WHEN…

Author Unknown

Just one peanut butter and jelly sandwich doesn't do it any more.

Driving a car doesn't always sound like fun.

The average ten-year-old doesn't have a clue who Bo and Luke Duke are.

Being bad is no longer cool.

You have friends who have kids.

Saturday mornings are for sleeping.

You are taller than the slide at the McDonald's playland.

Your parents' jokes are now funny.

You have once said, "Whatch-you talkin' 'bout Willis?"

You have owned, and since disowned Michael Jackson's Thriller.

Christmas starts to piss you off.

You would rather wear your dirty clothes again, 'cause mom is not there to do your laundry anymore.

Two words: parachute pants

Naps are good.

Hitting girls is no longer considered flirting.

You have once deemed Space Invaders as "The best game ever".

When you know that the machines in gas station bathrooms don't dispense balloons.

When things go wrong, you can't just yell, "Do-over!"

The only thing in your cereal box is...cereal.

You actually buy scarves, gloves, and sunscreen.

Your idea of fun parties now include Chips 'n' Salsa and Snapple.

You leave concerts and ballgames early to beat the crowd.

You WANT clothes for Christmas.

You don't want a Camaro because of the insurance premiums.

You remember when Saturday Night Live was funny.

You've bought an album on vinyl.

You remember seeing Star Wars when it first came out.

You read the "if you were born on this day in 1976 you are of legal age to buy alcohol" sign at the liquor store and recall attending a school dance on that date.

- 12 -
WISDOM

Life is like a mirror and will reflect back to the thinker what he thinks into it.
Ernest Holmes

N0TABLE QUOTES

Life is like riding a bicycle. You don't fall off unless you plan to stop pedaling.
Claude Pepper

When one door is shut, another opens.
Miguel de Cervantes

If you think you can, you can. And if you think you can't, you're right.
Mary Kay Ash

There are no shortcuts to any place worth going.
Beverly Sils

Happiness makes up in height for what it lacks in length.
Robert Frost

Winners never quit and quitters never win.
Vince Lombardi

Nothing is so embarrassing as watching someone do something that you said couldn't be done.
Sam Ewing

The future has a way of arriving unannounced.
George will

Success is getting what you want. Happiness is liking what you get.
H. Jackson Brown

UNKNOWN AUTHORS

Man's many desires are like the small metal coins he carries around in his pocket. The more he has, the more they weigh him down.

Survival strategy: "Laugh whenever you can, cry whenever you need to, appreciate the little things in life, and learn to roll with the punches.

The best way to have what you want, is to want what you have.

Spend your life lifting people up, not putting people down.

When there is a hill to climb, don't think that waiting will make it smaller.

Every person that you meet knows something you don't; learn from them.

Remember that the more you know, the less you fear.

Don't burn bridges. You'll be surprised how many times you have to cross the same river.

Until you make peace with who you are, you'll never be content with what you have.

Failure is an event. It is not a person.

Never Let Yesterday Use Up Today.

WORDS OF WISDOM

Self – Esteem is not what you think of yourself or what others think of you, but rather what you think other people think of you.
Unknown

Life is 10% of what happens to you and 90% how you react.
Unknown

It takes seven positive thoughts to replace each negative one.
Denis Waitley

If your personal security comes from within yourself, no one can ever steal it!
Stephen Covey

CREATIVITY IS:

- The ability to look at the same thing as everyone else and see something entirely different.

- A fragile and delicate state of mind that is profoundly affected by our interactions with others.
Authors Unknown

THE WISDOM OF EMERSON

Grow angry slowly – there's plenty of time.

The only way to have a friend is to be one.

A friend may well be reckoned the masterpiece of nature.

Health is the condition of wisdom, and the sign of cheerfulness, - an open and noble temper.

Our greatest glory is not in never failing but in rising up every time we fail.

Though we travel the world over to find the beautiful, we must carry it with us or we find it not.

What you do speaks so loudly that I cannot hear what you say.

Life is not so short but there is always time enough for courtesy.

This day is all that is good and fair. It is dear, with its hopes and invitations, to waste a moment on the yesterdays.

Write in your heart that every day is the best day of the year.

Adopt the pace of nature: her secret is patience.

A little praise goes a great ways.

THE WISDOM OF MARK TWAIN

Be respectful to your superiors, if you have any.

When angry count four; when very angry, swear.

Between believing a thing and thinking you know is only a small step and quickly taken.

Change is the handmaiden Nature requires to do her miracles with.

A thing long expected takes the form of the unexpected when at last it comes.

Happiness ain't a thing in itself--it's only a contrast with something that ain't pleasant.

Sanity and happiness are an impossible combination.

You can't depend on your judgement when your imagination is out of focus.

Supposing is good, but finding out is better.

Nature knows no indecencies; man invents them.

It is better to read the weather forecast before we pray for rain.

If you tell the truth you don't have to remember anything.

HENRY DAVID THOREAU

The man is the richest whose pleasures are the cheapest.

Don't waste the years struggling for things that are unimportant. Don't destroy your peace of mind by looking back, worrying about the past.

Live in the present, enjoy the present.

If one advances confidently in the direction of his dreams, and endeavors to live the life which he has imagined, he will meet with a success unexpected in common hours.

I you have built castles in the air, your work need not be lost; that is where they should be. Now put the foundations under them.

Why should we be in such desperate haste to succeed, and in such desperate enterprises? If a man does not keep pace with his companions, perhaps it is because he hears a different drummer.

When I hear music, I fear no danger. I am invulnerable. I see no foe. I am related to the earliest times, and to the latest.

The most I can do for a friend is simply to be a friend.

Live your beliefs and you can turn the world around.

DID YOU KNOW?

Men can read smaller print than women can; women can hear better.

Coca-Cola was originally green.

It is impossible to lick your elbow.

The state with the highest percentage of people who walk to work: Alaska

The percentage of Africa that is wilderness: 28%

(now get this...)
The percentage of North America that is wilderness: 38%

The cost of raising a medium-size dog to the age of eleven: $6,400

The average number of people airborne over the US any given hour: 61,000

Intelligent people have more zinc and copper in their hair.

The world's youngest parents were 8 and 9 and lived in China in 1910.

The youngest pope was 11 years old.

The first novel ever written on a typewriter: Tom Sawyer.

Those San Francisco Cable cars are the only mobile National Monuments.

Each king in a deck of playing cards represents a great king from history:
Spades - King David,
Hearts - Charlemagne,
Clubs -Alexander, the Great
Diamonds - Julius Caesar

111,111,111 x 111,111,111 = 12,345,678,987,654,321

If a statue in the park of a person on a horse has both front legs in the air, the person died in battle. If the horse has one front leg in the air, the person died as a result of wounds received in battle. If the horse has all four legs on the ground, the person died of natural causes.

Only two people signed the Declaration of Independence on July 4th, John Hancock and Charles Thomson. Most of the rest signed on August 2, but the last signature wasn't added until 5 years later.

Hershey's Kisses are called that because the machine that makes them looks like it's kissing the conveyor belt.

Q What occurs more often in December than any other month?
A. Conception.

Q. Half of all Americans live within 50 miles of what?
A. Their birthplace

Q. Most boat owners name their boats. What is the most popular boat name requested?
A. Obsession

Q. If you were to spell out numbers, how far would you have to go until you would find the letter "A"?
A. One thousand

Q. What do bulletproof vests, fire escapes, windshield wipers and laser printers all have in common?
A. All invented by women.

Q. What is the only food that doesn't spoil?
A. Honey

In Shakespeare's time, mattresses were secured on bed frames by ropes. When you pulled on the ropes the mattress tightened, making the bed firmer to sleep on. Hence the phrase "goodnight, sleep tight."

It was the accepted practice in Babylon 4,000 years ago that for a month after the wedding, the bride's father would supply his son in-law with all the mead he could drink. Mead is a honey beer and because their calendar was lunar based, this period was called the honey month we know today as the honeymoon.

In English pubs, ale is ordered by pints and quarts. So in old England, when customers got unruly, the bartender would yell at them mind their own pints and quarts and settle down. It's where we get the phrase "mind your P's and Q's"
Many years ago in England, pub frequenters had a whistle baked into the rim or handle of their ceramic cups. When they needed refill, they used the whistle to get some service. "Wet your whistle" is the phrase inspired by this practice.

In Scotland, a new game was invented. It was entitled Gentlemen Only Ladies Forbidden.... and thus the word GOLF entered into the English language.

At least 75% of people who read this will try to lick their elbows.

MORE THOUGHTS

Every teenager should get a high school education, even if they already know everything.

Health nuts are going to feel stupid someday, lying in hospitals dying of nothing.

Have you noticed since everyone has a camcorder these days no one talks about seeing UFOs like they use to.

You know when you're sitting on a chair and you lean back so you're just on two legs then you lean too far and you almost fall over but at the last second you catch yourself? I feel like that all the time.

According to a recent survey, men say the first thing they notice about a woman are their eyes. And women say the first thing they notice about men is they're a bunch of liars.

Whenever I feel blue, I start breathing again.

All of us could take a lesson from the weather. It pays no attention to criticism.

Why does a slight tax increase cost you two hundred dollars and a substantial tax cut save you thirty cents?

I'm not 40-something. I'm $39.95, plus shipping and handling.

In the 60's people took acid to make the world weird. Now the world is weird and people take Prozac to make it normal.

How is it one careless match can start a forest fire, but it takes a whole box to start a campfire?

Doctors can be frustrating. You wait month-and-a-half for an appointment, and he says, I wish you'd come to me sooner.

You read about all these terrorists: most of them came here legally, but they hung around on these expired visas, some for as long as 10-15 years. Now, compare that to Blockbuster; you are 2 days late with a video and those people are all over you. Let's put Blockbuster in charge of immigration.

MORE POINTS TO PONDER

Author Unknown

How can you tell when you run out of invisible ink?

Could someone ever get addicted to counseling? If so, how could you treat them?

Can you be a closet claustrophobic?

Did Adam and Eve have navels?

Does anyone ever vanish with a trace?

How does the guy who drives the snowplow get to work in the mornings?

If a turtle doesn't have a shell, is he homeless or naked?

If Fed Ex and UPS merge, would they call it Fed UP?

If a chronic liar tells you he is a chronic liar do you believe him?

If a mute child swears, does his mother wash his hands with soap?

If a tree falls in the forest and no one is around to see it, do the other trees make fun of it?

If all those psychics know the winning lottery numbers, why are they all still working?

If nothing ever sticks to TEFLON, how do they make TEFLON stick to the pan?

If olive oil comes from olives, where does baby oil come from?

What would a chair look like if your knees bent the other way?

If pro is the opposite of con, is progress the opposite of congress?

If quitters never win, and winners never quit, who came up with, "Quit while you're still ahead?"

If the Energizer Bunny attacks someone, is it charged with battery?

If you have a bunch of odds and ends and get rid of all but one of them, what do you call it?

What did we do before the Law of Gravity was passed?

What happens if you get scared half to death twice?

Why are we afraid of falling? Shouldn't we be afraid of the sudden stop?

Why do airlines call flights nonstop? Don't they all stop eventually?

Why is the alphabet in that order?

Why isn't phonetic spelled the way it sounds?

You know how most packages say "Open here" What is the protocol if the package says, "Open somewhere else?"

You know that little indestructible black box that is used on planes, why can't they make the whole plane with the same substance?

Sooner or later, doesn't EVERYONE stop smoking?

How do you know when it's time to tune your bagpipes?

Why are there Braille signs on drive-up ATM's?

THE POSITIVE SIDE OF LIFE

Author Unknown

Living on Earth is expensive, but it does include a free trip around the sun every year.

How long a minute is depends on what side of the bathroom door you're on.

Birthdays are good for you; the more you have, the longer you live.

Happiness comes through doors you didn't even know you left open.

Ever notice that the people who are late are often much jollier than the people who have to wait for them?

If Walmart is lowering prices every day, how come nothing is free yet?

Some mistakes are too much fun to only make once.

Don't cry because it's over; smile because it happened.

We could learn a lot from crayons: some are sharp, some are pretty, some are dull, some have weird names, and all are different colors....but they all exist very nicely in the same box.

A truly happy person is one who can enjoy the scenery on a detour.

PROVERBS & COUNTER-PROVERBS

Author Unknown

Actions speak louder than words.
The pen is mightier than the sword.

Look before you leap.
He who hesitates is lost.

Many hands make light work.
Too many cooks spoil the broth.

Clothes make the man.
Don't judge a book by its cover.

Nothing ventured, nothing gained.
Better safe than sorry.

The bigger, the better.
The best things come in small packages.

Absence makes the heart grow fonder.
Out of sight, out of mind.

What will be, will be.
Life is what you make it.

Cross your bridges when you come to them.
Forewarned is forearmed.

What's good for the goose is good for the gander.
One man's meat is another man's poison.

With age comes wisdom.
Out of the mouths of babes come all wise sayings.

The more, the merrier.
Two's company; three's a crowd.

ACKNOWLEDGEMENTS

The following were provided and printed with permission from:
www.GCFL.net
TOP TEN THINGS YOU'LL NEVER
HEAR A DAD SAY
THINGS YOU'LL NEVER HEAR FROM MEN
MY MOTHER TAUGHT ME...
THE THINGS CHILDREN SAY
WE LOVE OUR KIDS, KINDA
LAWS OF THE TODDLER
GETTING INTO HEAVEN
MY BROTHER'S BOOTS
HOW (NOT) TO SPEAK ENGLISH PROPERLY
OCCUPATIONAL DESCRIPTIONS
MORE THOUGHTS
MORE POINTS TO PONDER
THE POSITIVE SIDE OF LIFE
PROVERBS & COUNTER-PROVERBS

FRIENDSHIP BY MARCUS BROWN Provided by MidLink Magazine, Published by SAS inSchool, NC State University, and the University of Central Florida.

ABOUT THE AUTHOR

Russ Ulmer lives in Nebraska with his wife, Amy and two Basset Hounds, Dexter and Rainy. He is retired (somewhat).
He can be reached by email at rulmer1961@gmail.com

Russ Ulmer is available for public appearances and speaking engagements.. Having a fundraising program? Russ is always willing to be a part of your fundraiser, sign books and donate a portion of book sales to your organization. $5 from every book sold will be donated to your charity. Just contact him by email.

If you'd like to contribute a story (humorous or serious), quote or poem, just email them.

www.ingramcontent.com/pod-product-compliance
Lightning Source LLC
La Vergne TN
LVHW050643100826
148LV00011B/1957
0979331305 *